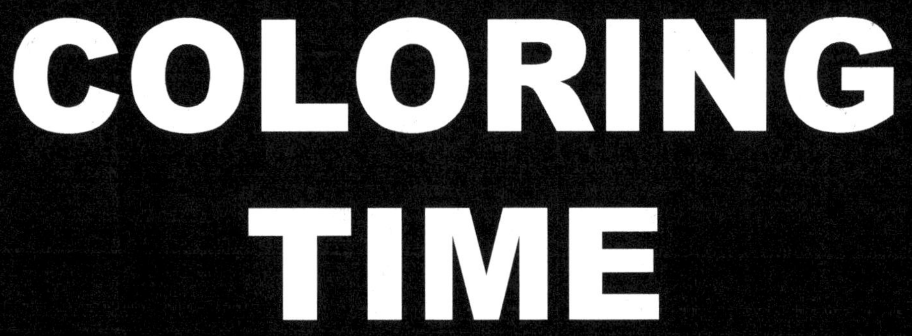


An Exhibition from the Archive of Korean - American Artists

Part One

(1955 - 1989)

# COLORING TIME

## An Exhibition from the Archive of Korean - American Artists

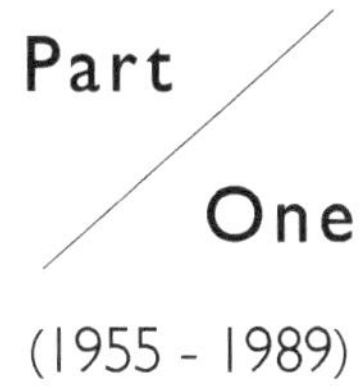


(1955 - 1989)

Kyunghee Pyun, Editor

AHL FOUNDATION, INC.

Published by
AHL Foundation, Inc.
420 West 23rd Street, Suite 7A
New York, New York 10011



This publication is issued in conjunction with the exhibition "Coloring Time: An Exhibition from the Archive of Korean-American Artists, Part One, 1955-1989," held at the Korean Cultural Service New York from April 10 through May 17, 2013.

The exhibition was collaborated by the AHL Foundation and Korean Cultural Service New York.

The exhibition is made possible in part by the Department of Cultural Affairs of New York City. Additional assistance has been received from Overseas Koreans Foundation.

Organized by *Kyunghee Pyun*
Designed by *Jieun Yim*

ISBN - 10: 1934717266
ISBN - 13: 978 - 1934717264

Printed in the United States of America

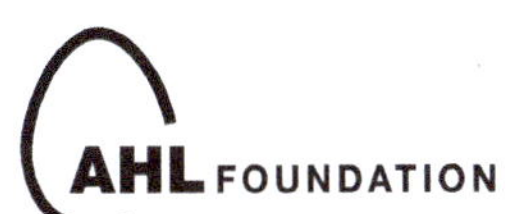

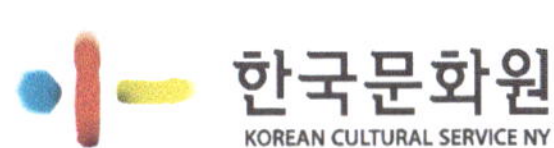

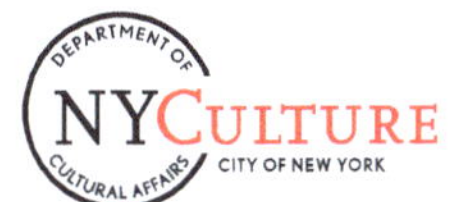

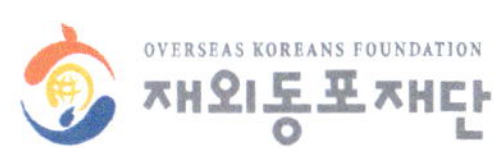

# CONTENTS



# APPENDICES

# DIRECTOR'S FOREWORD

The Korean Cultural Service New York (KCSNY) was founded in 1979 and celebrated its thirtieth anniversary in 2009. The Gallery Korea of the KCSNY was created in 1985, and has organized many exhibitions for Korea or Korean-American artists. Korean contemporary art has become quite prominent in the City of New York in recent years thanks to large-scale exhibitions of Korean artists, such as the retrospectives of Nam June Paik and Ufan Lee at the Guggenheim Museum, respectively, in 2000 and 2011, or the solo exhibition of U-Ram Choe at the Asia Society in 2011. In the last fifty years, more than several hundred Korean artists have come to New York to fulfill their ambitions. Some have left; others have remained. Po Kim, who arrived in New York in the 1950s, was one of the earliest Korean artists to come to New York. He was followed by Whanki Kim, Nam June Paik, and others in the 1960s.

It became apparent to many people when the first generation of those Korean-American artists began to die that efforts should be made to preserve and classify documents and materials related to Korean or Korean-American artists abroad. Those who went back to Korea or set up a studio in Korea could be included in the archives of Korean artists at the National Museum of Contemporary Art, Korea. On the other hand, Korean-American artists active in the United States can become part of the Archive of American Art at the Smithsonian Institute in Washington. But until our living artists become part of history, records and traces of their activities need to be preserved and collected.

It is fortunate that the AHL Foundation, a not-for-profit visual art organization founded by Ms. Sook Nyu Lee Kim in 2003, took the initiative on this ambitious project. Since 2010, President Kim conceived of a way to make the archive of Korean-American artists accessible to the public. Coloring Time is the first installment of a series of exhibitions to present a survey of the Cultural Service's archival materials.

KCSNY would not have been able to present its exhibition at Gallery Korea without the public's continuing support and the enthusiastic participation of artists. Almost all the Korean-American artists who arrived in the United States from the 1950s to the 1980s were willing to present their early works to the public in this exhibition. As director of KCSNY, I am overwhelmed by their interest in this project. Many artists took the time to collect old photographs and catalogues in the midst of their busy schedule with solo exhibitions and global tours. Thus, I wish to express both my personal appreciation as well as the gratitude of our institution to Korean-American artists who have supported this project.

At the Korean Cultural Service of New York, I wish to thank Ms. Hee-sung Cho, curator of Gallery Korea and co-curator of Coloring Time, who forged a new and exceptional rapport with Dr. Kyunghee Pyun and President Sook Nyu Lee Kim at the AHL Foundation. Dr. Soojung Hyun, researcher of the Archive of Korean-American Artists, was instrumental in securing key loans that have significantly enhanced the richness of the exhibition. Dr. Kyunghee Pyun, co-curator of the exhibition, created its intellectual framework in partnership with Ms. Cho and Dr. Hyun.

Lastly we are indebted to the leadership of President Kim of the AHL Foundation. I commend her for her commitment to the Archive of Korean -American Artists and for her ability to secure financial resources for the exhibition.

To all those involved as part of the artistic community of Koreans oversees, I extend my deepest appreciation.

Woo Sung Lee
Director
Korean Cultural Service, New York

# A MESSAGE FROM THE PRESIDENT

The AHL Foundation is honored to be able to collaborate with Gallery Korea of the Korean Cultural Service NY. My special thanks go to the director of the Korean Cultural Service NY, Mr. Woo Sung Lee, and to the curator of Gallery Korea, Ms. Hee-sung Cho for their dedication and enthusiasm. Upon hearing my plan to organize an exhibition along with a long-term project of collecting and classifying archival materials for the Archive of Korean-American Artists, Director Lee and Curator Cho became strong supporters of the project. I am grateful for their generosity and open-mindedness. As co-curator of this exhibition, Ms. Hee-sung Cho shared with us valuable materials among old documents and records kept at the Korean Cultural Service of New York.

I hope whole-heartedly that this exhibition will generate more interest in Korean contemporary art and continuous support for the Archive of Korean-American Artists. Dr. Soojung Hyun approached me a few years ago to create this project to preserve and document records of Korean-American artists. As a gallery owner in the 1980s, I was sympathetic to any attempt to enhance the recognition of these artists in the art world. During the preparation for this exhibition, Dr. Hyun and Dr. Kyunghee Pyun, co-curator of the exhibition, educated me on the scope and validity of the Archive of Korean-American artists.

Among numerous Korean-American artists who responded with overwhelming enthusiasm to our request to provide materials for the archive, Mr. Sung-ho Choi deserves special thanks from me and our staff. His meticulously organized documents, folders, photographs, reviews, and catalogues have our admiration. A great many of the materials displayed at the exhibition were loaned or donated by Mr. Choi. His generosity and expertise deeply impressed me.

I am deeply indebted to all the foundations including the Asia Art Archive in America and Asian American Arts Centre, galleries, art institutions, government agencies in New York and in Korea, and individual sponsors of the exhibition whose support have made this innovative exhibition a dream fulfilled. Mr. Robert Tully at the Korean Art Society was a strong believer in our project and lent his materials for the exhibition. The New York City Department of Cultural Affairs has been of tremendous help in our coming this far. Our many thanks also go to Ms. Christine C. Quinn, City Council Speaker of New York City for her visionary support of Korean contemporary art.

The entire AHL Foundation staff, as always, are to be thanked for their patience and supportive assistance whenever the need arose. Ms. Jongsook Ko and Mr. Wonseok Choi, assisted the curators in creating a directory of Korean-American artists; they also helped organize documentary sources and photographs in a folder for each artist. Jieun Yim, our graphic designer, also provided useful advice on the production of this exhibition catalogue. I also would like to express my gratitude to the board of trustees of the AHL Foundation for their everlasting support and assistance. Ms. Eun-young Kang, the Chair of the board, personally contacted prominent art collectors of Korean contemporary art to secure some key loans. I thank her for taking the initiative on that. Dr. Wolhee Choe, advisor to the AHL Foundation also contributed so much to the exhibition and to the ongoing project of the Archive of Korean-American Artists. We have been fortunate indeed to have all these supportive people helping to make this exhibit a reality.

Sook Nyu Lee Kim
President
The AHL Foundation

# INTRODUCTION

Kyunghee Pyun

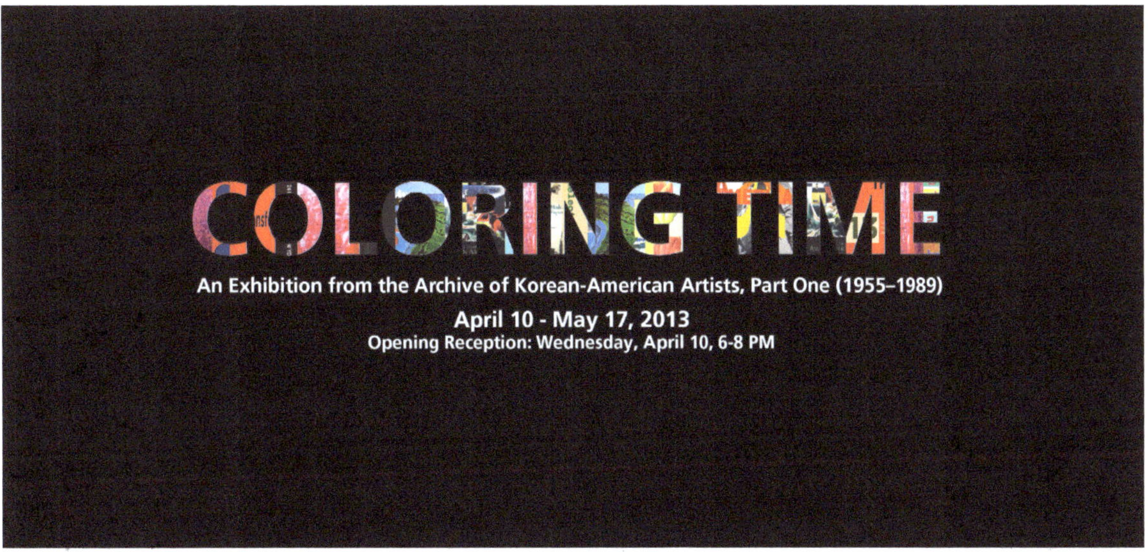


**Figure 1.**
Poster of *Coloring Time: An Exhibition from the Archive of the Korean-American Artists, Part One (1955-1989)* by AHL Foundation and Korean Cultural Service (2003) ©AHL Foundation Archive of Korean-American Artists

When I began my participation in the Archive of Korean American Artists project, I did not realize there were so many Korean artists. According to unofficial figures, the estimate is that more than two thousand Korean artists have been living and working in the New York area. For the first part of the project, the AHL Foundation and the Korean Cultural Service of New York decided to work with an older generation of artists, say those who arrived in New York or in the United States from the 1950s to the 1980s. That explains the long exhibition title *Coloring Time: An Exhibition from the Archive of Korean-American Artists, Part One (1955 –1989)*. *(Fig.1)*

Ideally Korean or Korean-American artists active in places other than New York should be contacted and included in this exhibition, but realistically it is not practicable. Unlike the Korean peninsula, American territory is too vast. For example, we know of artists in California and Washington DC, but we are completely ignorant of those who may be in Texas or Oklahoma. We decided to focus on New York where the largest number of Korean-American artists have lived and worked although some well-known artists in other regions may be mentioned. We also limited the time period to those who arrived before 1989, but the exhibition includes their activities up to 1999 in order to show the first few years right after the MFA degrees. This is not a major retrospective of Korean-American artists as a group but an exhibition as part of the Archive of Korean-American Artists. In fact many artists sent us documents and records of their art works rather than the actual art works. Still we are fortunate to be able to include many seminal art works from their early careers, and we have accumulated a sizable amount of biographical data.

In the beginning of the project, we sent a questionnaire to all the artists on our list to identify those arriving before 1989, and many of them returned the form, evincing interest in this exhibition. Among these artists, we contacted and interviewed about three dozen Korean artists who arrived between 1955 and 1989. Many of them were still living in the New York area. Po Kim was still actively working on his large-scale oil paintings. Unfortunately, Whanki Kim and Nam June Paik had passed away. Among a younger generation, Mi-ae Moon, Wonjun Park, and Mo Bahc are also no longer alive. Byungki Kim retired to California, so we were unable to meet with him for this exhibition. Yong-jin Han, the husband of the late Mi-ae Moon, also left New York and retired to Jeju Island, Korea. A few of the older artists proved to be of great value for us because they had kept in touch with younger colleagues through their affiliation with Hong-ik University or Seoul National University, two of the oldest higher-education institutions with fine arts programs.

On difficult issue that came up was whether to include Korean artists who stayed only briefly in the United States, either to earn their degrees or for other reasons. Tchang-yeul Kim (1929– ) studied at the Art Students League from 1966 to 1968, and then went to Paris, encouraged by Nam June Paik. Kwang Young Chun (1944– ) studied at the Philadelphia College of Art and exhibited his works at commercial galleries in New York, Philadelphia, and the Delaware area in the 1970s. Soo-cheon Jheon (1947– ) came from Japan to New York to study at the Pratt Institute in the late 1970s. We finally decided to distinguish between those who immediately went back to Korea after receiving a degree, and those who did not, including several artists who stayed and worked here five years beyond their schooling.

As an historical project, we wanted to discover more Korean artists who were aspiring at one time during their life but not widely known to Korean news media or art communities. Robert Han (Kisuk Han; 1930– ) or called "Nong" was a self-taught artist based in San Francisco. He never went to a fine arts program in Korea or in the United States. His creative works drew admiration first here and then later in Korea. But for the most part, we did not have enough time or resources to research artists outside the New York area. The Archive of Korean-American Artists will continue to document activities of Korean or Korean-American artists on the West Coast, in the Midwest, or in the South . Unlike Korean artists in Europe, Korean artists in this country are part of a large community of Korean immigrants. Like other immigrant groups, Korean-Americans have become assimilated. Eventually some of them will be remembered as part of American art— as Nam June Paik is considered "father of video art" in the history of contemporary art. We hope our exhibition attracts much interest in the diverse, multicultural aspects of Korean contemporary art and honors prescient, yet striving Korean artists in the second half of the twentieth century. It is natural that the accomplishments and activities of these artists become part of the artistic heritage of Korea. Simultaneously, each of them also deserves to be a glitzy piece in the mosaic of American art history—perhaps global art.

Before the 1960s, aspiring and talented artists in Korea aspired to go to Paris, the center of artistic activities[1]. With a romantic view of an artist's life, Paris was "the place" for an artist to be. In the 1940s and 1950s some Korean artists were fortunate enough to live and work in Paris. Lee Ungno (1904–1989), for example, a renowned ex–patriot artist trained in Korean and Japanese ink painting left for Paris in 1958, and presented collage works using handmade Korean paper and other pigments under contract with the Facchetti Gallery from 1961 to 1964.[2]

After Japanese colonialism ended in 1945, American military power was still a strong presence in Korea. During the Korean War, some Korean artists began going to the United States, either as a student or an exchange fellow through a growing tie between the two countries. Political confusion and ideological confrontation forced some artists to take refugee. Po Kim (1917– ) left Korea after a painful ordeal during civil unrest in the southwestern region in Korea. When he arrived at the University of Illinois at Urbana-Champaign, Kim discovered a new trend in art: abstract art. In comparison to Po Kim, Ki Suk Han (known as Han Nong) worked in the American Embassy in Korea and then studied international public law at University of Michigan in the 1950s. As a self-taught artist, Han Nong opened his own gallery in Oakland in 1963 and later in San Francisco.[3]

Whanki Kim (1913–1974), on the other hand, was a more cosmopolitan painter. Having studied with the department of fine arts at Nihon University (1933–1937), he taught fine arts at Seoul National University from 1948–1950, and then at Hong-ik University from 1952–1955, and then again from 1959–1963. An abstract artist, as seen by his 1938 work, *Rondo* at the National Museum of Contemporary Art, he was aware of international trends. He first went to Paris to develop a mature style and absorb new trends. During his stay in Paris from 1955 through 1958, he discovered that subjects or motifs from Korean traditional art were favored by international audiences. *(Fig. 6)* He went to Brazil to represent Korea at the Sao Paolo Biennale in 1963.*(Fig. 4)*

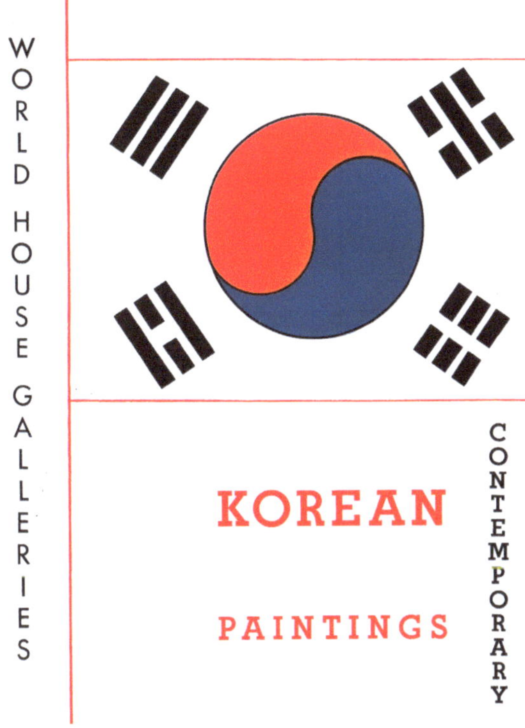


**Figure 6.**
Exhibition Catalogue of *Contemporary Korean Paintings* at World House Galleries in New York, 1958. Collection: Mr. Robert Turley

On the way back, he visited New York and saw the potential of the city as a new center for visual arts. *(Fig. 3)* He settled in New York in 1963 until his premature death in 1974. His style evolved, and he developed the famous blue dots lined up vertically and horizontally, more reminiscent of Eastern ink painting than Western abstract art.

Both Po Kim and Whanki Kim became aware of the new, abstract style of painting, and like their compatriots in Paris, enjoyed the freedom of experimenting and developing new artistic languages. *(Fig. 5)* Soon they were followed by a group of younger Korean artists. Yong-jin Han, Mi-aie Moon, and Byoung Ok Min came to New York. Unlike Whanki Kim and Po Kim, who learned fine arts in Japan, these young artists

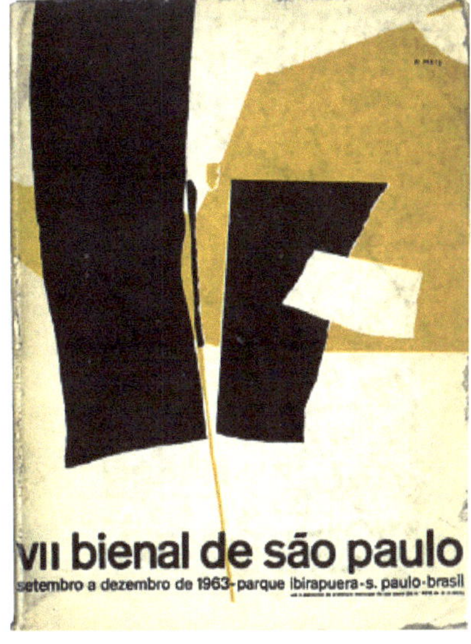


**Figure 4.**
Poster of San Paulo Bienal, 1963.
Collection: Mr. Robert Turley

were educated in the university system in Korea. They came to New York with professional aspirations to be familiar with new artistic trends and be known to a wider group of audiences.

As an immigrant group in this country, Korean artists were a fraction of all the Korean immigrants. Between 1955 and 1959, about forty-five hundred Koreans immigrated; from 1960 to 1964 over nine thousand people immigrated. In total, between 1955 and 1964, out of about fifteen thousand Korean immigrants, an overwhelming majority were either Korean women married to American soldiers or Korean children adopted by American families[4)].

In the 1960s, many Korean artists went abroad and developed a new style called *Art Informel*. As the French term represents, most of these artists identified their style with a new breed of French artist focusing on monochrome, abstract paintings. Likewise, Korean artists in New York were also participating in abstract art although their works were somewhat different from the abstract expressionism of American artists in the 1950s. Korean artists displayed a more intellectual, formally controlled look of abstract art.

Some artists earned MFAs at American art institutions and went back to Korea, but a few artists did not go back. These artists set tled in New York or some other large American city. Their professional success did not come easy. A limited number of art galleries and cultural institutions were interested in contemporary art.

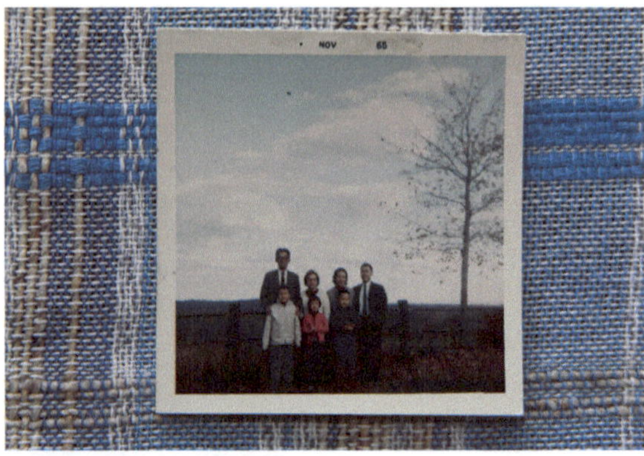


**Figure 3.**
Photograph of Whanki Kim and Matthew Kim (collector and medical doctor) with their family in New York, 1965. Collection: Dr. Matthew Kim

Considering that American contemporary art received little or scant attention from the public, it is not difficult to imagine how hard immigrant artists had to work to prove the quality of their work. A language barrier and cultural differences made things even more difficult. Herbert Mayer's World Art Gallery held an exhibition of the works of Korean artists in 1958. Other than that, there were no major shows. Some Korean artists had individual contacts with American gallery owners. John Pai and Byoung Ok Min, who went to Pratt Institute for their MFA degrees in the 1960s, started to make their presence known in New York art galleries.

One exceptional artist, Nam June Paik, spent his youth in Japan in the 1950s and studied music in Germany in the early 1960s. With his family's wealth and cultural enrichment from Europe, Paik became a strong presence in the New York art scene as part of the Fluxus movement in the mid-1960s and remained influential as a pioneering figure in video/installation art while other Korean artists who were active in the 1960s lived in a more isolated world of their own.

In the 1970s the world opened up a bit more to Korean artists. A larger number of talented, aspiring artists "chose" to come to New York because it was the center of artistic creativity. Educated by art professors who themselves had studied abroad, these young artists—mostly from Hong-Ik University and Seoul National University— were ambitious to be recognized

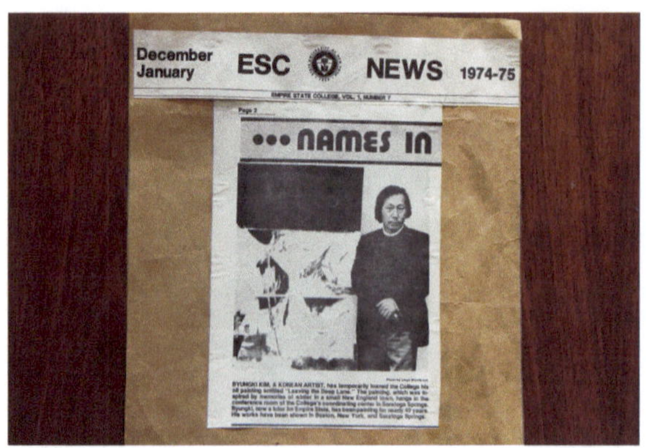

December January ESC NEWS 1974-75

••• NAMES IN

**Figure 5.**
Byungki Kim in Empire State College Newspaper, 1974/75. Collection: Chong Yun Kim

outside their own country[5]. Unlike artists in the 1960s, most of them enrolled at various MFA programs around the country. Because of their access to American art schools and partly because of the excellent quality of their work, those who arrived in the 1970s presented their works at commercial galleries more easily. At the same time, the art world grew more interested in and receptive to non-Western artistic traditions. Many immigrant artists said they discovered the beauty and meaning of their own cultural heritage on foreign soil. Encouraged by this intellectual atmosphere for anti-establishment and non-European sentiment during the civil rights movement and the protest against the Vietnam War, Korean artists in turn developed techniques and subject matter to satisfy the demands of American and European audiences. Some artists exhibited geometric or purely formal shapes in appearance—reminiscent of minimalism for example, but they claimed to have been inspired by traditional Korean culture or Asian philosophies. While Korean artists at home wanted to emphasize their compatibility with global art scenes, Korean artists abroad made efforts to exploit "Koreanness" in their works. It was an admirable attempt. Because of the cultural policies of the Japanese colonial government, those generations born in the 1920s and 1930s were not educated with a coherent, positive outlook to embrace the historical and cultural legacy of Korea, and thus did not cultivate a cultural identity. The experience of living abroad in turn strengthened the urgency of Koreans to discover their legacy of being Korean.

The artistic atmosphere stimulated by the civil rights movement and multiculturalism in this country was favorable to these intellectual, "cerebral" Korean artists.

In the 1980s more and more Korean artists came to America. It is partly due to an abrupt political change in Korea and its subsequent policy to loosen up certain restrictions. The military dictatorship continued from 1961 to 1987, so many intellectuals including artists settled in America as a place of temporary refuge[6]. As many Korean immigrants arrived for various roles in the American economy, scores, if not hundreds, of Korean artists or art students came to pursue their MFA degrees at American art institutions. Nonetheless, feminism and the civil rights movement did not have much impact on Korean artists although they were aware of these movements. A younger generation of artists showed interest in combined painting and conceptual art while some attempted performance art and raised awareness of public art. Artists who arrived in the 1980s, as well as older artists who were settled in, pursued more recognition in the context of multiculturalism. *(Fig. 7)* They continued to study Asian

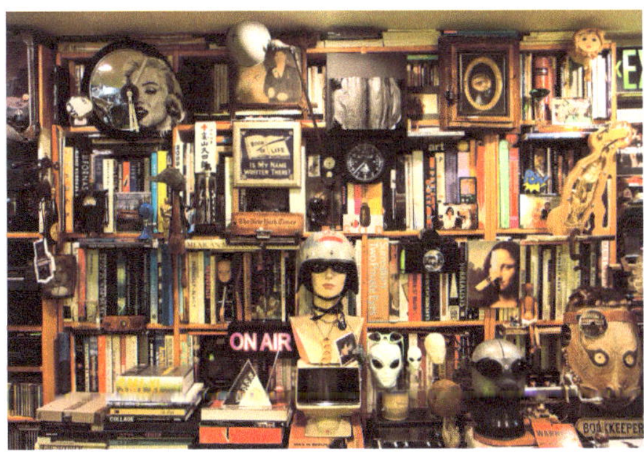


**Figure 7.**
Chong Gon Byun's Library/Apartment in Brooklyn, 2013. ©AHL Foundation Archive of Korean-American Artists

philosophies, develop subject matters unique to their cultural heritage, and expand their techniques in such areas as calligraphy and Korean ink painting.

This trend is related to the American and European interest in art works from different parts of the world. Several major exhibitions on Asian art continued with porcelain, ink painting, and decorative arts from the early modern period as represented by exhibition titles such as *Traditional Korean Pottery; Contemporary Korean Painting and Asian Traditions/Modern Expressions: Asian American Artists and Abstraction,* 1945–1970[7] *(Fig. 8)*. Art critics and essayists wanted to discover "unique" art works distinguished from well-known American or European artists. For example, they did not want to discover another Jackson Pollock from Korea or China. When they organized exhibitions of contemporary art works, they selected art works often described as or associated with "Eastern philosophy." Korean artists in Korea were aware of this. So were Korean artists here. In fact American art critics and curators were eager to discover Korean artists in Korea rather than those active here. Important exhibition focusing on contemporary Korean art included the work of more Korean artists in Korea than in America.

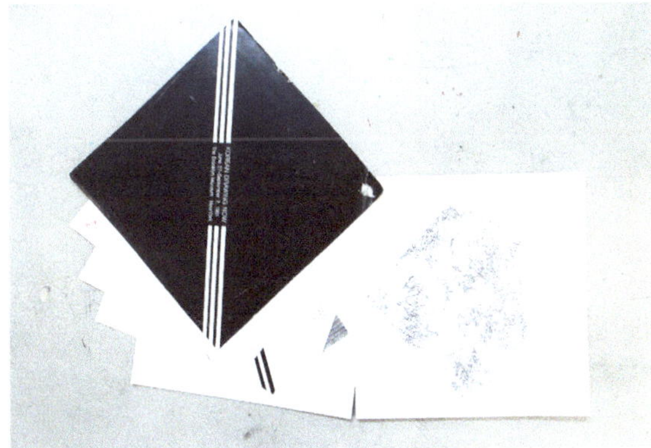

**Figure 8.**
Exhibition Catalogue of *Korean Drawing Now* at Brooklyn Museum, 1981/82. Collection: Sung Ho Choi

In the late 1980s and the 1990s, contemporary Koreanart started to be displayed in large-scale exhibitions. The Korean Cultural Service of New York opened the Gallery Korea and regularly displayed the work of Korean or Korean-American artists. The Queens Museum of Art, Asia Society, Harlem Studio Museum, and the New Museum organized several major exhibitions of Asian-American art in which Korean or Korean-American artists were included.

A few galleries in the 1980s were actively promoting Asian or Korean artists; by that time Koreans also owned galleries. In the 1990s a few Korean artists were invited to participate in the Whitney Biennale and also showed their work at the Whitney Philips. Korea participated in the Venice Biennale in 1995[8], and Jheon Soocheon, who represented Korea in 1995, was educated at the Pratt Institute in the 1980s. Ik-joong Kang, in 1997, was a Korean-American participant artist, as were Michael Joo and Do ho Suh in 2001 as well as Sooja Kim in 2005. All had spent a critical period in their career in New York.

In this catalogue, Deborah Saleeby-Mulligan presents a sketch of notable art movements and figures in New York from 1955 through 1999. Korean artists in the United States were aware of the trends or flows of contemporary art, but they did not actively participate in the 1960s. Later in the 1970s and especially in the 1980s, Korean artists organized more group exhibitions with fellow Korean artists or Americans. In addition, they were often invited to group exhibitions and international art fairs in Korea and also abroad. In my essay on the activities of Korean artists from 1955 to 1989, I focus on group exhibitions or exhibitions of Korean artists held at American art institutions and galleries. In the archive of Korean-American Artists, there are records of many Korean artists exhibiting in Korea and abroad. There are numerous materials, so the exhibition and the catalogue concentrate more on depicting Korean art accomplishment in America.

The last essay by Soojung Hyun discusses Korean and Korean-American artists in the 1990s, and expresses their engagement with society in the form of public art or organized groups.

It should be noted that Korean artists spell their names in a variety of ways. Some insist that their last name come before the first name, unlike the American style. Korean first names are often hyphenated, so part of the first name could be mistaken for a middle name in English. We did our best to follow the preference of the artist in deciding how each first name would appear in the exhibition catalogues and other publications. But we followed English convention for consistency in publication, by always placing the last name at the end. Readers and artists alike need to bear this in mind.

I sincerely hope that our first exhibition will generate the interest in Korean-American artists they so clearly deserve. Such a beginning would favor the opening of the second exhibition on artists arriving in the 1990s and 2000s, and the third exhibition on artists outside New York would proceed with even greater participation and success. Asian Art Archive (AAA) based in Hong Kong and Brooklyn and a Digital Archive of Asian/Asian-American Contemporary Art History at the Asian American Arts Centre (AAAC) include some materials on Korean-American artists. Several Korean-American artists will be part of the Archives of American Art at Smithsonian Institution. The Archive of Korean-American Artists (AKAA) can be another valuable research center to recognize and reevaluate contributions of artists of Korean heritage. In addition, the National Museum of Contemporary Art in Korea collects and classifies archives of Korean contemporary art in the archive team within its curatorial department. Eventually the Archive of Korean-American Artists will be an indispensable repository of information on a dynamic and accomplished group of artists of Korean or Korean-American heritage. An intellectual trend in which American institutions of higher education and postgraduate research now encourages Asian-American studies in association with history, politics, art, literature, music, film, law, ethics, and other traditional fields will further sustain the raison d'être of the Archive of Korean-American Artists. This is a work in progress, but will accrue tremendously in the coming years along with the sincere support of the art community of Koreans in the United States.

# NOTES

1) Youngna Kim, *Modern and Contemporary Art in Korea: Tradition, Modernity, and Identity* (Elizabeth, NJ and Seoul: Hollym), 2005.

2) Youngna Kim, *Modern and Contemporary Art*, 31.

3) Gordon H. Chang et al., *Asian American Art: A History, 1850–1970* (Palo Alto, CA: Stanford University Press, 2006), 402. It is notable that this book came out from Stanford Asian American Art Project.

4) Pyong Gap Min, ed., *Asian Americans: Contemporary Trends and Issues* (London: SAGE Publications, 2006), 232. In 1975–1979, a dramatic increase of immigrants added more than 155,000 people. In 1975–1989 the number of Korean immigrants peaked and declined in numbers since 1990. See fig. 10. 1 in his book.

5) Whanki Kim and other well-known artists teaching at Seoul National University and Hong-ik University participated in international art exhibitions. Also, Soojai Lee (1933– ) received Institute of International Education Scholarship to the University of Colorado, Boulder and studied under Carl Morris. After receiving her MFA degree in 1958, she went back to Korea and taught at the College of Fine Arts, Ewha Woman's College. Chun Sung-woo (1934– ), after attending Seoul National University in 1953, went to San Francisco State College and San Francisco Art Institute in 1955, received his MFA at Mills College in Oakland, California in 1960 and then a Ph.D. in art history at Ohio State University in 1964. He briefly taught at the Richmond School of Art in California in 1964–65 and went back to Korea. He taught at the College of Fine Arts at Seoul National University from 1968 to 1971.

6) Pyong Gap Min, "Korean Americans" in *Asian Americans*, 232–233.

7) Traditional Korean Pottery; Contemporary Korean Painting was an exhibition held at Sarah Lawrence College Art Gallery in Bronxville, New York in 1982 (curator: Kyu-nam Han) while *Asian Traditions/Modern Expressions: Asian American Artists and Abstraction, 1945–1970* was shown at Jane Voorhees Zimmerli Art Museum, Rutgers University, New Brunswick, NJ, March 23–July 31, 1997.

8) Japan started to have their own pavilion and show their artists at the Venice Biennale since 1952.

# NEW YORK ART TRENDS 1955-1999

by Deborah Saleeby-Mulligan

The second half of the twentieth century was a time of rapid change in American art. Between 1955 and 2000, the New York art world experienced such an accelerated pace of transition that each decade seemed to mark a fundamental shift in artistic style and practice. Artists actively began to move away from the traditional Modernist categories of painting and sculpture by creating new contemporary work that redefined the nature of art, its creation, reception, and theoretical underpinnings. Contemporary New York art aggressively challenged standards of public taste and often reflected the cultural and sociopolitical changes that were sweeping the country. One can point to several key developments in the New York art world that radically transformed art making in the country and arguably throughout the globe. This essay is not meant to be a comprehensive history of New York Contemporary art between 1955 and 2000, but rather offers a general overview of the period by focusing on the history of several groundbreaking exhibitions, the influential critical literature of the time, and the work of the period's most significant artists.[1)]

At the onset of the Second World War, New York became a magnet for modern European artists who were seeking a safe haven from the war. Among the celebrated artists who came to New York were Piet Mondrian, Marcel Duchamp, Hans Hofmann, and Max Ernst. These artists in exile influenced a young generation of American painters and sculptors, later known as the New York School artists. Their style of abstract expressionism was the first major American style to gain international influence[2)]. In May 1951, the exhibition "9th Street Show," organized in large part by the art dealer, Leo Castelli, featured seminal work by the abstract expressionist artists, Willem de Kooning, and Jackson Pollock, and also included the work of the younger artist, Robert Rauschenberg.[3)]

By 1955, abstract expressionism was canonized into the history of modernism[4)]. Art theorists Clement Greenberg and Michael Fried championed abstract expressionism for its formal purity, and they marginalized all other art styles in an effort to promote work that, as Greenberg stated, was "uninflated by illegitimate content.[5)]" Greenberg and his disciple Fried negated the sociopolitical context of the art in favor of the creation of an optical art that was stripped of subject matter and detached from the mundane world. Others, such as art critic Harold Rosenberg and artist Allan Kaprow, viewed abstract expressionist work as inherently performance based. In 1953, Rosenberg coined the term "action painting." He theorized that the new style of painting had become "an arena in which to act." He further noted that "what was to go on the canvas was not a picture but an event.[6)]" In 1956, after the untimely death of Jackson Pollock, Allan Kaprow, one of the forerunners of performance art, challenged young artists to expand the boundaries of abstract expressionism. Kaprow believed that through his inherently 'performative' action, Pollock had dissolved the art of painting and extended the creative process of art into the larger environment[7)]

Allan Kaprow and Claes Oldenburg were among the next generation of New York artists who sought to blur the boundaries between art and life. They pioneered the performance-based art form and coined the term "happening" to refer to a theatrical interactive art which eliminated the barrier between the performer and the audience. In a happening the audience was forced to participate in the action. Many of the happenings took place in the alternative art space, the Judson Gallery in Greenwich Village. The gallery was also important for showcasing the work of artists who would later be associated with the pop art movement, such as Tom Wesselmann and Jim Dine.

Many New York artists working in the late 1950s were inspired by the Dada artist/provocateur

Marcel Duchamp. Beginning in the second decade of the twentieth century, Duchamp rejected what he called "retinal art" in favor of work that was put in the "service of the mind." In 1957, Duchamp delivered an influential lecture in the United States titled the "Creative Act." In this lecture he noted that art is not performed by the artist alone but is fundamentally linked to the experience of the spectator[8]. Duchamp's theories and particularly the iconoclastic impulse of his readymade work became the inspiration for much of the groundbreaking art created by John Cage, Robert Rauschenberg, and Jasper Johns during the 1950s, and successfully promoted by the art dealer Leo Castelli at his Upper East Side gallery.[9]

John Cage, although primarily a composer and musician, was one of the pioneers of performance art. His infamous composition 4'33," first performed in 1952, incorporated the sounds of the audience. Cage stimulated the emergence of the Fluxus movement. His important role as a mentor and teacher was disseminated through his teaching positions at both Black Mountain College in North Carolina and The New School for Social Research in New York. In 1956, Cage met and befriended Naim June Paik. Paik's video sculptures, inspired by Cage, and his later experiments in television art expanded the parameters of the Fluxus movement. During the 1960s, the Fluxus artists in New York included George Maciunas, Yoko Ono, and George Brecht. Their work was often performed in New York's Soho neighborhood at the Fluxhall at 359 Canal Street. In their avant-garde performances, these artists revealed their debt to Duchamp's theories on art, specifically the importance placed on the role of the spectator and how that person completed the work of art and assigned it meaning.

The mainstream art world of the 1960s was still very much grounded in the traditional medium of painting. The style most popular among New York art dealers, critics, and museums was post-painterly abstraction exemplified by the work of Helen Frankenthaler, Morris Louis, and Kenneth Noland. Their work was heralded by Greenberg who believed this next generation of painters was extending the possibilities established by Pollock and the abstract expressionists through works that were aesthetically pure.[10]

The mainstream style of minimalism also embraced this notion of purity. The geometric abstractions of the minimalist painters and sculptors of the late 1950s and early 1960s, such as Ad Reinhardt, Donald Judd, and Frank Stella were promoted in influential exhibitions at the Green Gallery, Pace Gallery, and the Leo Castelli Gallery. Castelli was also the first New York art dealer to bring attention to the work of the pop artists. In the early 1960s his gallery was the first to exhibit the comic-inspired images of Roy. Lichtenstein and the Coca-Cola bottles and the Campbell's soup cans of Andy Warhol. In 1962, the renowned Sidney Janis gallery organized the exhibition "The New Realists," which brought pop art to a wider audience.[11] Although initially derided by critics for its derivative qualities and commercial imagery, pop art quickly became accepted by the mainstream art establishment.[12]

The 1970s was a tumultuous decade in the New York art world. The artwork of this time was highly confrontational and often reflected the ideals of civil rights, women's rights, and the anti-Vietnam War movements. Many artists reacted negatively to the market value placed on their art and attempted to circumvent the gallery system by creating work that was nonobjective and dematerialized. This resulted in the emergence of several styles, including, conceptual art, earth art, and body art (which was often informed by feminist art practice).

Conceptual art, like the earlier Fluxus movement, had its roots in Duchampian theory. Most conceptual artists distrusted the privileging of object-based art forms and intentionally sought to avoid the commercialization of their work. Conceptual artists in New York such as Joseph Kosuth and Lawrence Weiner created language-based work that in the words of Kosuth, was "a shift from the perceptual to the conceptual ... a shift from the physical to the mental." [13] Art critic Lucy Lippard noted that conceptual art led to the dematerialization of art. The idea presented took precedence over the physicality of the object itself. [14]

By 1971 many female artists began producing work that was informed by feminist ideology in an effort to challenge the mainstream art world's exclusion of women and feminine subject matter. The feminist intervention into the visual arts transformed the art world and led to its expansion to include artists concerned with issues of race and identity. New York-based artists such as Carolee Schneemann, Hannah Wilke, and Nancy Spero pioneered work that sought to heighten political awareness of women's issues. Female artists organized feminist galleries and collective spaces such as the Artists in Residence Gallery (AIR).

The anti-establishment spirit of the feminist art movement that began in the 1970s influenced a growing number of street artists who came to prominence in the 1980s. Young artists like Jean-Michel Basquiat and Keith Haring created vibrant paintings reflecting the disaffected spirit of street culture.[15] Haring, a graduate of the School of Visual Arts, gained fame for his subway drawings; he would later co-opt the pop aesthetic and brilliantly market his own work. Basquiat was catapulted to fame after his 1980 "Time Square Show," which gained the attention of the art dealer Mary Boone. Boone created a superstar in Basquiat by aggressively promoting his work. Her gallery also established the career of painter Julian Schnabel and many others.

The culture wars of the 1980s culminated in several controversial art world events such as the destruction of Richard Serra's public sculpture The Titled Arc at Federal Plaza in New York. The work of artists such as Robert Mapplethorpe and Andres Serrano ignited a public debate regarding censorship in the arts after conservative members of the federal government called for the removal of funding for the National Endowment for the Arts.

On the heels of these contentious events, New York artists often produced overtly challenging work. Artists featured at the 1993 Whitney Biennial such as Charles Ray, Jimmie Durham, and Peon Osorio confronted notions of difference and personal identity. Controversy continued to preoccupy the art world up to the close of the twentieth century. In 1999, the Brooklyn Museum hosted the traveling exhibition "Sensation Young British Artists from the Saatchi Collection." The exhibition came under attack from New York Mayor Rudolph Giuliani, who criticized the work in the exhibit on the grounds that it was anti-religious. Although he never saw the exhibition, he threatened to cut public funding to the museum. The event stimulated a debate on the public value of art and the freedom of art institutions to exhibit works of their own choosing.

# NOTES

1) Sources on Contemporary Art include: Michael Archer, *Art Since 1960* (New York: Thames and Hudson, 2002); Hal Foster, Rosalind Krauss, Yves-Alain Bois and Benjamin H. D. Buchloh, eds., *Art Since 1990: 1945 to the Present*, vol. 2 (New York: Thames and Hudson, 2004). David Hopkins, *After Modern Art 1945-2000* (Oxford: Oxford University Press, 2000) Gill Perry and Paul Wood, *Themes in Contemporary Art* (New Haven: Yale University Press, 2004); Kristen Stiles and Peter Selz, eds., *Theories and Documents of Contemporary Art: A Sourcebook of Artists' Writings* (Berkeley: University of California Press, 1996); Brandon Taylor, *Contemporary Art Since 1970* (London: Laurence King Publishing, 2004).

2) The abstract expressionists were a loose group of artists who congregated in the Cedar Tavern in Greenwich Village. They heldweekly discussions and aesthetic debates at the Artist's Club, or 'The Club' located on East 8th Street.

3) See Dore Ashton, *The New York School* (Berkeley: University of California Press, 1992) and Marika Herskovic, *The New York School Abstract Expressionists: Artists Choice by Artists* (New York: New York School Press, 2000).

4) In 1958 The Museum of Modern Art organized the European touring exhibition "The New American Painting." The exhibit highlighted the work of the abstract expressionists and was largely responsible for disseminating the style internationally.

5) Clement Greenberg, "Our Period Style," *Partisan* Review, 16/11 (November 1949), 1138.

6) Harold Rosenberg, "The American Action Painters," *Art News*, 51/8 (December 1952), 22.

7) See Allan Kaprow, "The Legacy of Jackson Pollock," *Art News*, 60/3 (October 1958), 36-39; 58-62.

8) Arturo Schwarz, *The Complete Works of Marcel Duchamp* (London: Thames and Hudson, 1969), 149.

9) In 1961 the Museum of Modern Art showcased the work of Rauschenberg and Johns in the exhibition "The Art of Assemblage." William C. Seitz, *The Art of Assemblage*, exhibition catalog (New York: The Museum of Modern Art, 1961). See also Annie Cohen-Solal, *Leo and His Circle: The Life of Leo Castelli* (New York: Alfred A. Knopf, 2010).

10) Clement Greenberg, "Post Painterly Abstraction," in *Clement Greenberg: The Collected Essays and Criticism, Vol. 4: Modernism with a Vengeance 1957-1969* (Chicago: University of Chicago Press, 1993), 192-196.

11) Brian O'Doherty, "Pop goes the New Art," *The New York Times*, November 4, 1962, section 2, 23.

12) By 1963, The Museum of Modern Art had within their collection the *Gold Marilyn* by Andy Warhol.

13) Joseph Kosuth, "Four Interviews with Barry, Huebler, Kosuth, Weiner," *Arts Magazine* (February 1969), 22.

14) See Lucy Lippard and John Chandler, "The Dematerialization of Art," *Art International*, 12/2 (February 1968), 31-36.

15) Haring and Basquiat were part of the street culture of the impoverished East Village of the 1980s where numerous art galleries opened including the Fun Gallery and the Nature Morte. The East Village became fertile ground for many visual, film, and music artists.

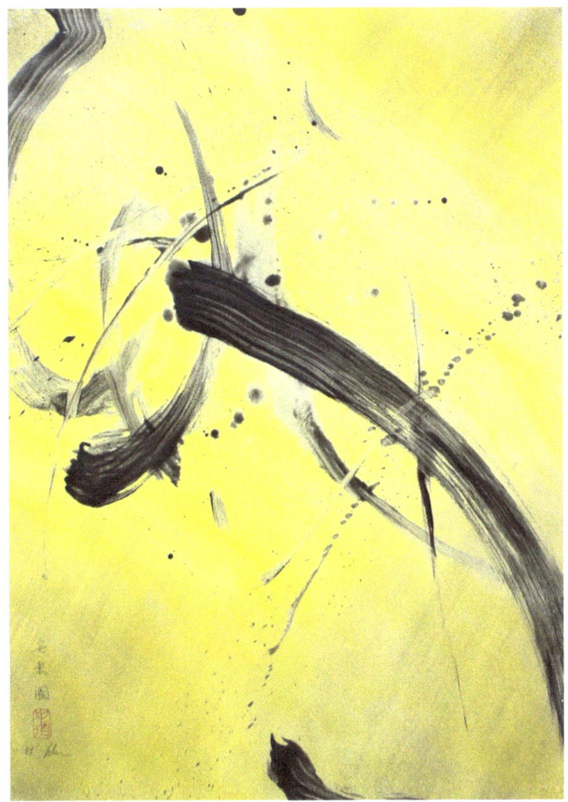

**Plate 1**
Dong Kuk Ahn(Don Ahn)
*Dragon in the Fog, 1997*
Acrylic on canvas, 28.5 x 21inches,
Collection : Artist

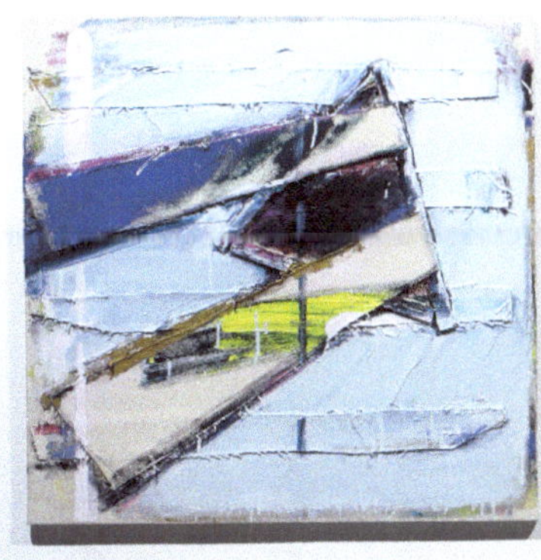
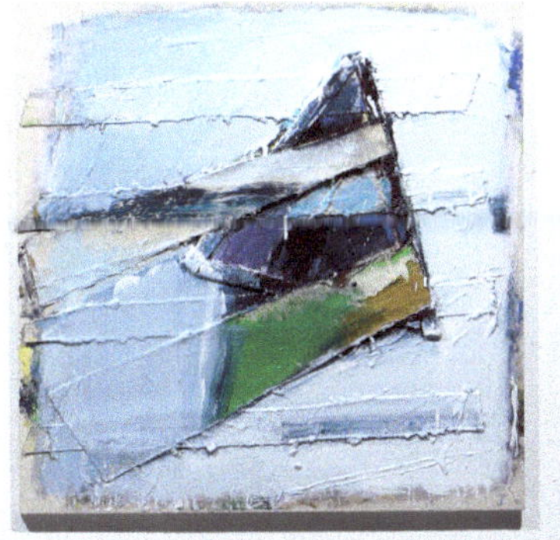

**Plate 2**
Byoung Ok Min
*Tide, 1998*(Diptych),
Wood, canvas strips, acrylic on canvas, 31x32 inches(each).
Collection : Artist

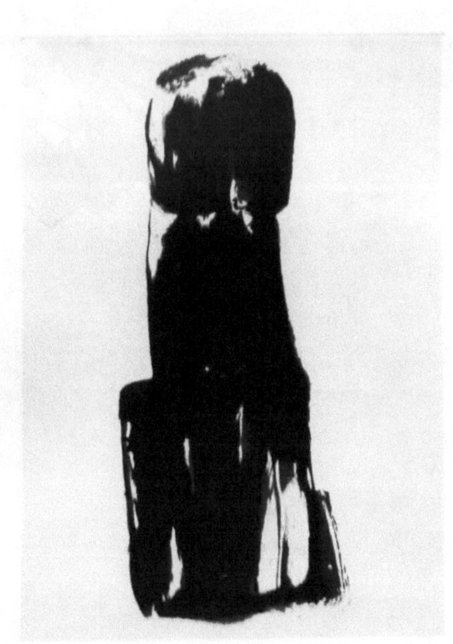

**Plate 3**
Han Yong Jin
*Untitled,* 1997
Lithograph on paper, 40x28 inches
Collection : Ahlfoundation, Inc.

# KOREAN-AMERICAN ARTISTS IN NEW YORK IN THE 1990s

Soojung Hyun

This essay illustrates some movements among Korean-American artists in New York during the 1990s. In the late 1980s, as well as the 1990s, postmodernism was an important cultural code that represented the multiplicity of artistic and intellectual expressions on class, gender, race, and sexuality. Of the postmodernism phenomena, multiculturalism and identity politics were catalysts for the recognition of Korean-American artists. *(Fig. 9)* A number of Korean-American artists in New York expressed their opinions regarding identity politics through their works at such visual arts venues as museums, cultural centers, alternative spaces, and galleries. *(Fig. 10 and 11)* One theme shared by many Korean-American artists concerned the issue of identity among immigrants. This theme brought these artists into a group to promote a progressive cultural movement among Korean immigrants and to network with other minority ethnic groups as part of the identity politics movement. Korean-American artists who were not part of the group developed their artistic careers by experimenting with various themes and aesthetics rather than identity issues. This study examines the types, themes, and venues of some major exhibitions in which Korean-American artists participated in the 1990s. Such information not only provides an insight to understanding the kind of art and the message that Korean-Americans artists pursued at that time, but also tracks their growth in the New York's art world.

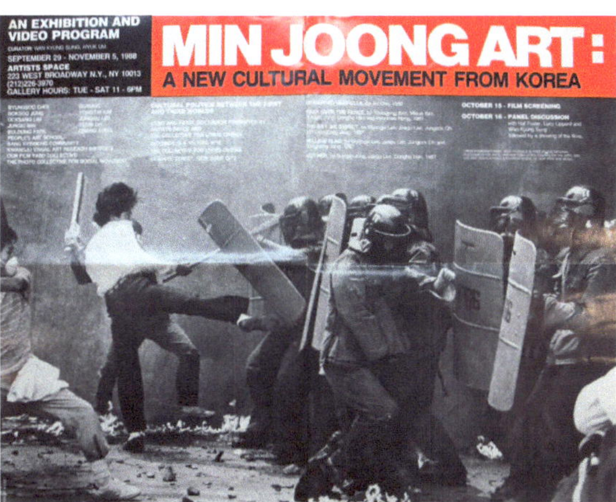


**Figure 9.**
Poster of *Min Joong Art* Exhibition, 1988. Collection: Sung Ho Choi

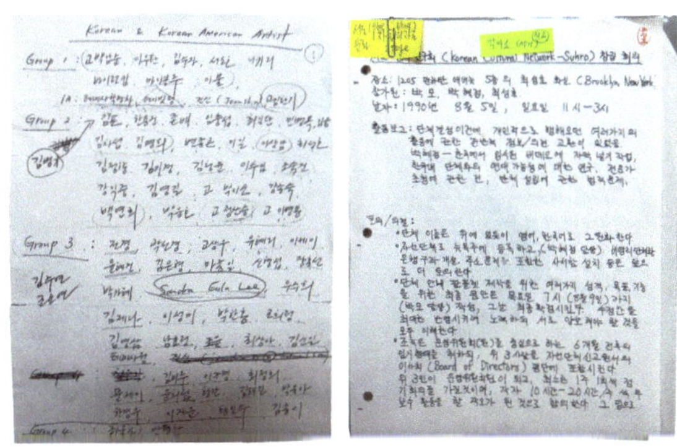

**Figure 10**
List of Names by SEORO Korean Cultural Network, 1990. Collection: Sung Ho Choi

**Figure 11.**
Foundation of SEORO Korean Cultural Network (handwriting by Yiso Park/Mo Bahc), 1990. Collection: Sung Ho Choi

A thematic exhibition entitled *The Decade Show: Frameworks of Identity in the 1980s* (May 12–August 19, 1990) addressed the issues of multiculturalism and identity politics. The exhibition was presented at three museums: the New Museum of Contemporary Art, the Museum of Hispanic Contemporary Art, and the Studio Museum in Harlem. This show was a provocative examination of artistic production in the 1980s, embracing ninety-four artists of Hispanic, Asian, African American, Native American, and European heritage. The exhibition's openness to diversity and its focus on the challenges of minorities provided a great opportunity for emerging Korean-American artists to showcase their work to the New York art world. Youngsun Min and David Chung were invited to participate in the show. The subject of their works reflected the life of minority immigrants; Min was particularly concerned about the issue of identity of the female immigrant.

Concomitant to *The Decade Show*, another meaningful exhibition was held in Brooklyn at the Center for Art and Culture of Bedford Stuyvesant (July 1–July 28. 1990) called *The Mosaic of the City: Artists against Racial Prejudice*. *(Fig. 12)* In comparison to *The Decade Show*, which covered a wide range of identity issues, this exhibition narrowed its focus to racial issues. The exhibition invited Asian-American, African American,

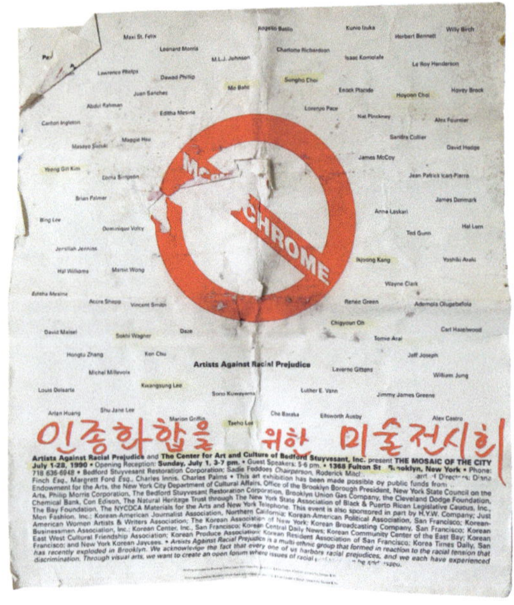


**Figure 12.**
Poster of *Mosaic of the City* Exhibition, 1990. Collection: Sung Ho Choi

Afro-Caribbean, and Hispanic artists. Korean-American artists Young Son Min, Mo Bahc, Sung Ho Choi, Tae Ho Lee, David Chung, Yeong Gill Kim, and Ho Yoon Choi were represented in this exhibition. It was the first time that the two major ethnic groups—African American and Asian—came together for a group show in a major art institution. Despite the racial tensions between the two groups (there was an African American boycott of the Korean-owned Red Apple grocery in Brooklyn), the exhibition promoted racial harmony, mutual understanding, and acceptance among various groups. In addition, *Public Mirror: Artists against Racial Prejudice* (September 13–October 17, 1990) demonstrated the same context as *The Mosaic of the City* at the Clock Tower Gallery in Queens. The artists who were invited to participate in this show held up a mirror, forcing viewers to confront racial prejudice and to share new perspectives.

These exhibitions raised questions about the ways in which multiculturalism had manifested itself in the arts. The mainstream New York art organizations embraced the change. In 1992 a Korean-American artist, David Chung, presented his work *Turtle Boat Head* (Charcoal on paper, Wood, metal, Plexiglas, Video installation 7.30 min.) representing immigrant life in urban America at the Whitney Museum of American Art (July 15–September 12, 1992). Ik-Joong Kang also presented his 3 x 3-inch work at Queens Museum of Art in 1992. Byron Kim contributed "Synecdoche" (1991–92) to the Whitney Biennial in 1993. David Chung and Byron Kim are both second generation Korean-Americans, and Ik-Joong Kang immigrated to the United States in 1984. Their works show that they've absorbed western ideas and expression techniques, yet still pursued their own artistic language, which is distinct from Western culture. Around this same period, more Korean-American artists started to debate the issues of identity and culture. These debate gatherings developed into the Korean-American artist group, the Seoro Korean Cultural Network.

The Seoro Korean Cultural Network was the pioneering artist group founded August 5, 1990 by Mo Bahc, Sung Ho Choi, and Hae Jung Park. They published a quarterly magazine *Seoro Seoro* (translated as "together and together")" (Fall 1991–Summer 1994). The Seoro Korean Cultural Network organized forums and promoted networking among Korean-American artists and other minorities outside mainstream American culture. One of their efforts resulted in a monumental exhibition *Across the Pacific: Contemporary Korean and Korean-American Art* (October 15, 1993– The exhibition featured solely Korean and Korean-American artists, thus distinguishing these artists from a larger group of Asian-American artists. The exhibition was also unique in showing the works of contemporary Korean artists working in Korea in addition to the Korean-American artists working in the United States. [1)]

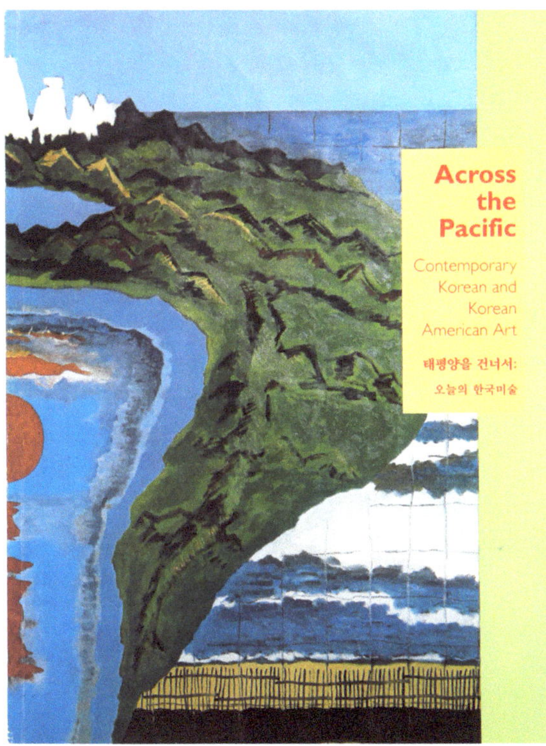


**Figure 13.**
Exhibition Catalogue of *Across the Pacific* at Queens Museum of Art, 1993/94. ©AHL Foundation Archive of Korean-American Artists

*Across the Pacific* was composed of three sections: the works of Korean artists, the works of Korean-American and Korean-Canadian artists, and the films and videos of Korean-American artists. Young Chul Lee from Korea organized the first section, and Jane Faver, the director of the Lehman College Art Gallery in the Bronx, organized the second section. Hye Jung Park and Christine Chang were in charge of the last section. Thirty-six artists were invited to exhibit their work. The exhibited works ranged from Korean traditional brush paintings to installation, film, and video works. *Across the Pacific* was a monumental exhibition in a number of ways. The art reflected the most prevailing social issues the artists face in their lives. For Korean-American artists, the critical social issues concerned the life of minorities and immigrants; for the Korean artists, the issues regarded governmental oppression.[2) ] In other words, the works of Korean-American artists reflected their individual's experiences and the hardships they faced to gain new artistic identities in the foreign land; while Korean artists mainly delivered a message regarding social issues and conflict in Korea[3)]. Another interesting difference between Korean-American and Korean artists was the style and aesthetic media used by the two groups. In comparison to Korean artists, who kept the style and aesthetic media of traditional Korean paintings, Korean-American artists followed the language and conceptual installation of western abstract painting.

The exhibition received much attention from the media and the public. Articles about the exhibition appeared in *The New York Times*, *Art in America*, *Daily News*, and Korean newspapers in New York and Korea[4)]. The exhibition stimulated a cultural discourse; "Beyond Boundaries," the first National Asian-American Arts Conference was held during the exhibition (December 19, 1993) at the Time and Life Building in New York City.

Following *Across the Pacific*, another exhibition entitled *Asia/America: Identities in Contemporary Asian American Art* opened at the Asia Society Galleries, New York (February 16–June 26, 1994). It continued the identity theme of Asian and Asian-American artists. The exhibition showed the works of twenty non-Western artists who came to the United States to live and work. Margo Machida organized the exhibition as a guest curator. *(Fig. 14)* A third-generation Japanese-American, she was born in Hawaii, the only state with an Asian majority. She came to New York in 1968, and her experiences in New York made her ponder the meaning of Asian identity in the United State. She categorized Asian-American identity issues into four broad areas: traversing cultures; situating; speaking to and of Asia; and addressing the interaction between the east and the west. These embrace many issues that Asian immigrants experience.[5)] The essays of the exhibition in the exhibition catalog were written by Margo Machida, Vishakha Desai, and John Tchen, and comprehensively analyze identity tensions, the experience of cultural displacement, and the construction of cultural identity. Participating artists were Asian-Americans with their roots in China, Japan, Korea (Young Son Min, Sung Ho Choi, David Chung and Jin Su Kim), the Philippines, India, Thailand, and few other Asian countries. The exhibition was reviewed as a well-organized exhibition that synthesized diverse art works and artists under the theme of multiculturalism and identity politics.

In the mid 1990s, exhibitions of Asian and Asian-American artists were continually held at other public venues. *Traditions / Tensions: Contemporary Art in Asia* opened at the Asia Society Galleries, Grey Art Gallery of New York University, and Queens Museum of Art (October 3, 1996–January 5, 1997). This mammoth exhibition presented contemporary Asian artworks by artists from India, Indonesia, Philippines, South Korea, and Thailand in one of the first large-scale pan-Asian exhibitions in New York. Similar to *Asia/America: Identities in Contemporary Asian American Art,* the exhibition adopted a broad multinational perspective. It brought together a diverse range of contemporary artworks from across the Asia region. The global aspect of the exhibition was reflected in that Korean artists from Korea were invited to participate in this exhibition (Jeong-Hwa Choi, Kim Sooja, Duck Hyun Cho), but Korean-American artists were not. This can be interpreted as the influence of the internationalization of Korean artists. In 1995, for the first time, Korea established the Korean pavilion in the Venice Biennale, and launched a global Biennale in Kwangju. The theme of these exhibitions focused on more contemporary experimental works of an international standard than on identity issues.

*In the Eye of the Tiger* composed of both Korean and Korean-American artists (May 28–July 5, 1997) focused on more contemporary experimental works. One theme of the artwork was the concept of individual ideas.[6)] Korean artists had been quick to embrace the new technologies of communication and the culture of mass media. The explosive mass-cultural feed of the new information age brought a new kind of awareness to formulate a personal artistic vision in an increasingly global society.

Looking back on the Korean-American art movement in 1990s history, Korean-American artists had to consider the problem of action and intervention in relation to the confluence of identities continually evolving outside their original cultural context. However as the identity issue ceased to be a central theme of the art world in the late 1990s, other issues were raised in the New York art world with globalism and the vitalization of the art market. A number of Korean-American artists who were not involved in the multiculturalism movement developed their careers through shows at well-known galleries such as the O. K. Harris Works of Art, Sandra Gering gallery, and the Howard Scott gallery in New York. Tchah-Sup Kim, Choong Sup Lim, Byong Ok Min, Woong Kim, Il Lee, Chong Gon Byun, Wonsook Kim, Jung Hyang Kim, Mikyung Kim, Young Gill Kim, and Sook Jin Jo focused on forms and ideas aligned with the Asian traditional spiritual aspect. These artists pursued more personal interests or aesthetic experiments. They became progressively more recognized in the art venues of New York, and their activities were followed by new generation of Korean-American Artists in the twenty-first century.

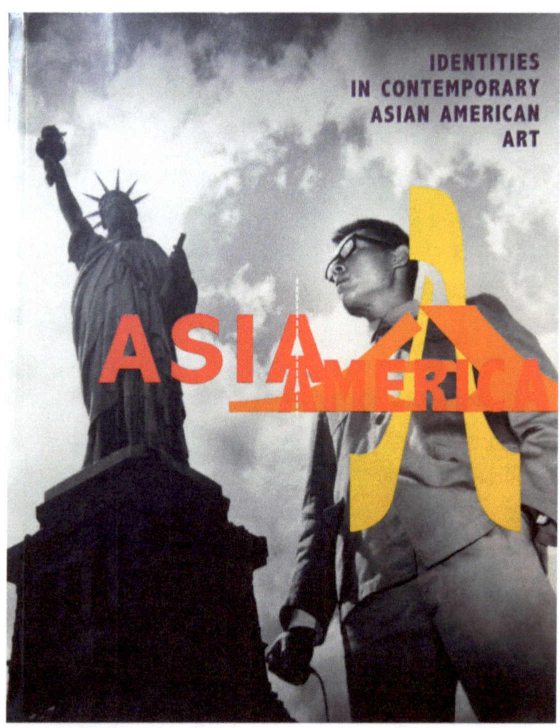


**Figure 14.**
Exhibition Catalogue of *Asia/America: Identities in Contemporary Asian American Art* at Asia Society Galleries, 1994.
©AHL Foundation Archive of Korean-American Artists

## NOTES

1) Alice Yang, "Looking for the identity of Korea Art", *Why Asia? : Contemporary Asian and Asian American Art,* edited by Jonathan Hay and Mimi Young (New York and London: New York University Press, 1998), 65

2) The section of Korean artist was especially characterized by the artwork related to Minjung Art, even though there were some other styles of Korean contemporary art. There was an exhibition to introduce about Minjung Art to New York. *Minjung Art: A new cultural movement from Korean* was held at Artist Space in New York from September 29 to November 5, 1988. It was a style of art movement in South Korean. Minjung Art revealed the miserable reality by Korean government's dictatorship and resisted the offensive controls to limit human freedom.

3) Young Chul Lee, "Culture in the Periphery and Identity in Korean Art," *Across the Pacific: Contemporary Korean and Korean American art* (New York: The Queens Museum of Art, 1993), 15. According to the curator of the Korean Artist section, Young Chul Lee explained about the composing of the show. The artist in exhibition Across the pacific can divided into the four groups: political artist bound by the total and collective, artists who agree on the critical perspective, artists who show gender issue, and artists who try to undermine modernism's presupposition.

4) Holland Cotter, "Korean Works Coming to Terms With the West," *New York Times*, December 10, 1993. *The New York Times* stated that this exhibition showed a distinction in depicting a central challenge of multiculturalism despite some curatorial restrictions.

5) *Asia/America: Identities in Contemporary Asian American Art* with essays by Margo Machida, Vishakha Desai, and John Tchen (New York: The Asia Society Galleries and The New Press, 1994), 68.

6) The exhibition at Exit Art in New York was composed by ten Artists: Tae Jin Yook, Sung Min Hong, Young Sun Lim, Dong Chun Yoon, Seung Teak Lee, Young Jin Kim, Choong Sup Lim, Sook Jin Jo, Myoung Hye Kim, and Hwa Young Park.

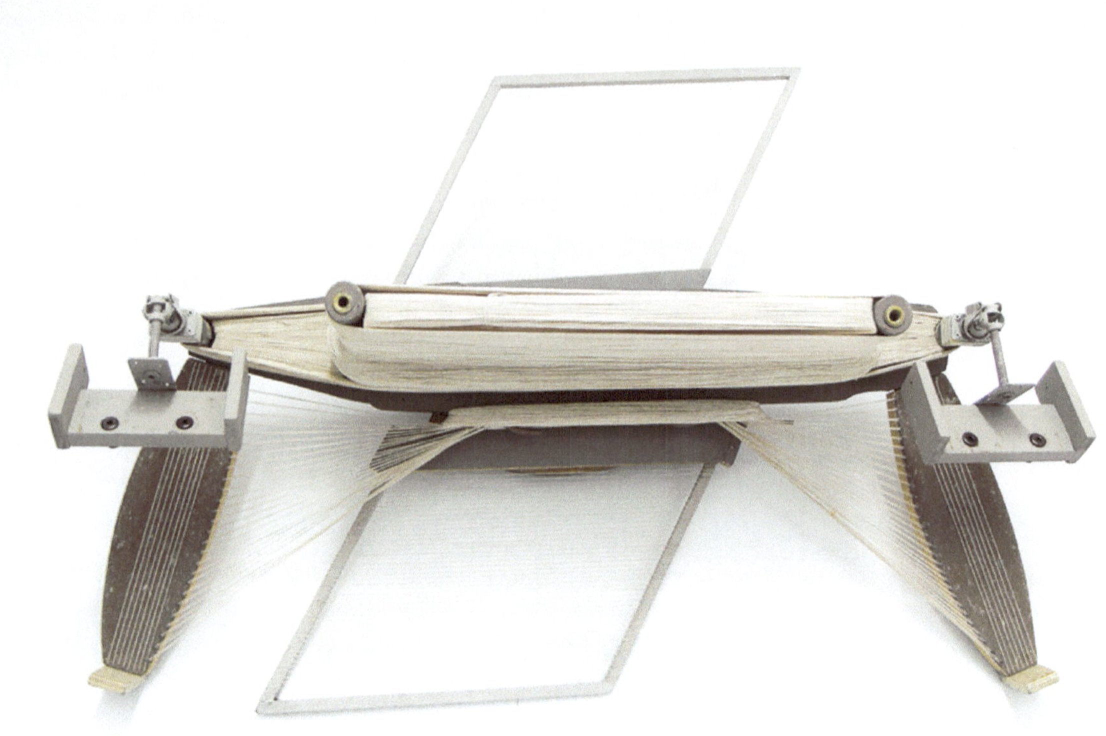

**Plate 4**
Choong Sup Lim .
*Ta - Rae (Spindle)*, 1995
Threads, acrylic, wood, rice paper, U.V. L. S gel, 32 x 45 x 15 inches .
Collection: Artist

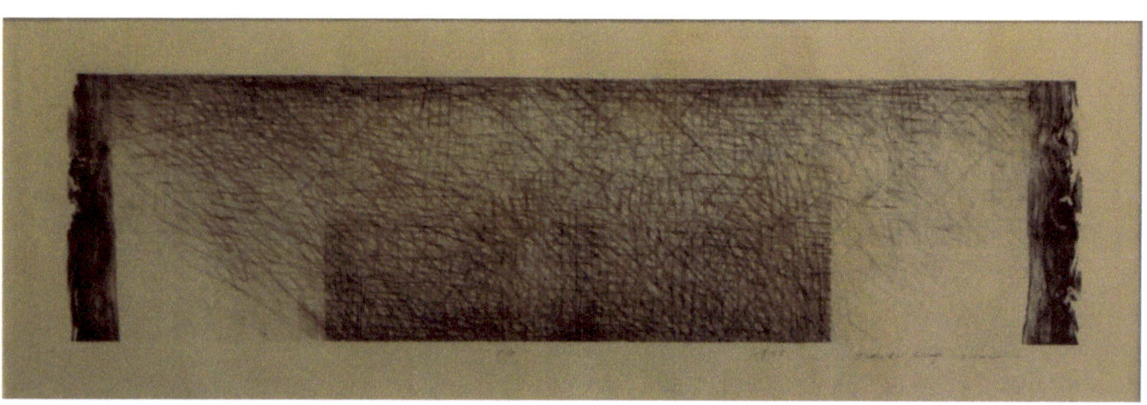

**Plate 5**
Tchah Sup Kim
*Untitled, 1975 .*
Etching print on paper, 9 x 29 inches
Collection: Artist

# A NOTE ON KOREAN - AMERICAN ARTISTS: TOWARD A NEW DEFINITION

Hee Sung Cho

As the curator of Gallery Korea at the Korean Cultural Service of New York, one of the questions most often asked is: How many Korean artists are currently working in New York? From what has been reported in the media, the number of Korean artists based in New York is upwards of two thousand. That is a huge figure: there is no other city in the world with such a high concentration of Korean artists. And if you go back to the early 1960s — about the time when Korean artists began to proliferate in New York — the story becomes more interesting and even more impressive. There are the trailblazers who began half a century ago and are still going strong; there are the artists who made a brief sojourn in the city before heading back to Korea or another country; there are those who displayed a burst of activity and then made a career change; and then there are those who unfortunately are no longer with us.

Most would agree that New York has been the focal point of the global art market since the Second World War. Thus it is not only a prestigious and coveted a venue for artists to inhabit, but it is a tough and competitive one. And the numerous Korean artists who have flocked to New York—whether in the 1960s, 1970s, 1980s, or even 2013 for that matter—did so with gritted teeth and a good many broken claws. And yet it has been voluntary, with brimming aspirations and a desire to pursue art. They have been passionate, radical, and unquenchable in their artistic drive. In discussing the history of contemporary Korean art, we therefore must consider the story of the American-based Korean artists: how they evolved and what kind of impact they wrought is an important thread in the overall narrative. As such, further research on this topic is necessary and should be expected.

The Archive of Korean-American Artists will be presented in three smaller installments rather than as a sprawling single show, mostly for reasons of limited time, space, manpower, and funding. Part 1, which is slated for this year, will cover information we have compiled on Korean artists who were on the scene in New York from the 1950s through the 1980s. For this exhibition Dr. Kyunghee Pyun and I managed to contact about thirty artists and collect a bulk of material that might otherwise have been lost or languishing in storage indefinitely.

As mentioned earlier, many of these artists are still alive and living in the New York area. Po Kim is still actively working on his large-scale oil paintings, but Whanki Kim and Nam June Paik have passed away. Among the younger generation, Mi-ae Moon, Wonjun Park, and Mo Bahc are no longer alive. Byungki Kim retired to California, so we could not meet with him for this exhibition. Yongjin Han, the dear husband of the late Mi-ae Moon, also left New York and retired to Jeju Island in Korea. But he generously contributed his time for this project. A number of senior artists have been of great value to us because of their continuing relationship with younger artists through their affiliations with Hong-ik University and Seoul National University, the two oldest higher-education institutions with fine arts programs in Korea.

A difficult issue for us was whether to include Korean artists who were in the United States only briefly, usually for their degree programs or for other reasons. Tchang-yeul Kim (1929– ), for instance, attended the Art Students League (1966–68) before setting out to Paris, encouraged by Nam June Paik. *(Fig. 2)* Kwang Young Chun (1944– ) studied at Philadelphia College of Art and showed his work at commercial galleries in New York, Philadelphia, and in the Delaware area in the 1970s. Soo-cheon Jheon

(1947– ) came from Japan to New York to study at the Pratt Institute in the late 1970s. We ultimately decided to include only those who stayed and worked in the United States for at least five years beyond their schooling.

As a historical project, we wanted to discover more Koreans who were committed to making art but were not generously covered in the Korean news media or were not widely known in art communities. Robert Han (Kisuk Han 1930– ), alternatively known as "Nong," is a self-taught artist based in San Francisco. Although he never matriculated in a fine arts program, nonetheless his work has garnered recognition over time, first here and later in Korea.

For the exhibition this time around, we did not have enough time or resources to survey artists outside the New York area. The Archive of Korean-American Artists will, however, go on to document activities of Korean or Korean-American artists on the West Coast, in the Midwest, and in southern regions. Compared to those, say, in Europe, Korean artists in the United States have led lives more typical of a Diaspora population; that is, they have assimilated while coalescing into a large community of Korean immigrants within this dynamic crucible of a country. Some of them may eventually be remembered as integral to American art, like Nam June Paik, who is considered the father of video art in the history of contemporary art.

We hope our exhibition will shine a new light on contemporary Korean art, and elicit much interest in the distinctly multicultural aspect of it. And, most of all, we pay tributes to those Korean nationals of the second half of the twentieth century who passionately and tenaciously pursued art, often in the absence of commensurate rewards commercially or otherwise. It is only reasonable that their accomplishments become part of Korea's artistic heritage. Simultaneously, each of them also deserves a proud place in the mosaic of American art history—or perhaps even in global art.

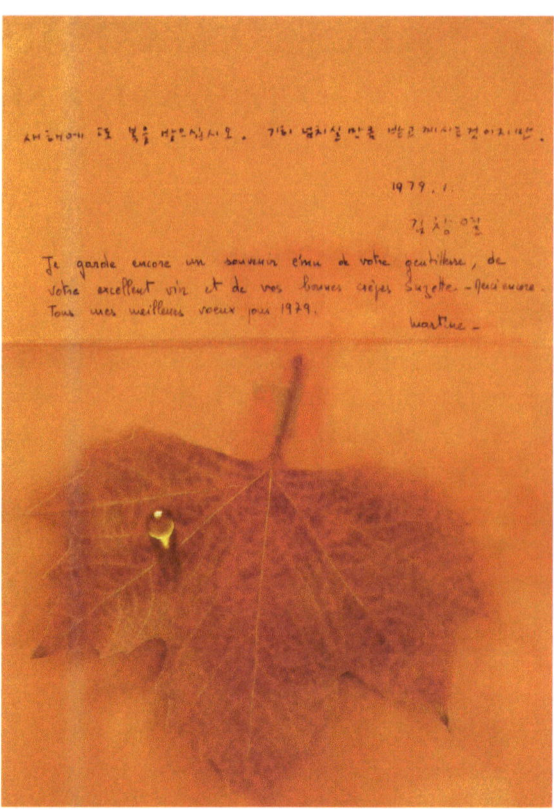

1979. 1.
김창열
Je garde encore un souvenir ému de votre gentillesse, de
votre excellent vin et de vos bonnes crêpes Suzette. - Merci encore.
Tous mes meilleurs voeux pour 1979.
Martine -


**Figure 2.**
Tchang-yeul Kim's Postcard to Collector Matthew Kim in New York, 1979.
Collection: Dr. Matthew Kim

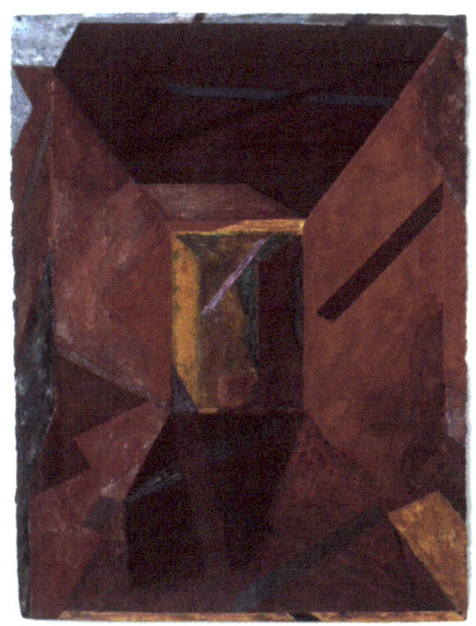
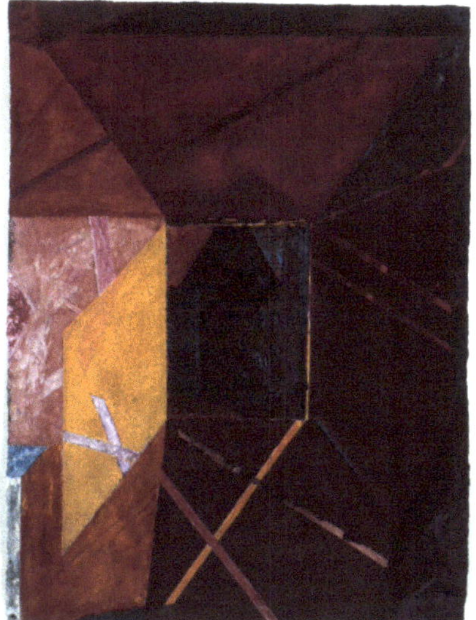

**Plate 6**
Woong Kim
*Red interior,* 1981
Oil on canvas, 29 x 44 inches
Collection: Artist

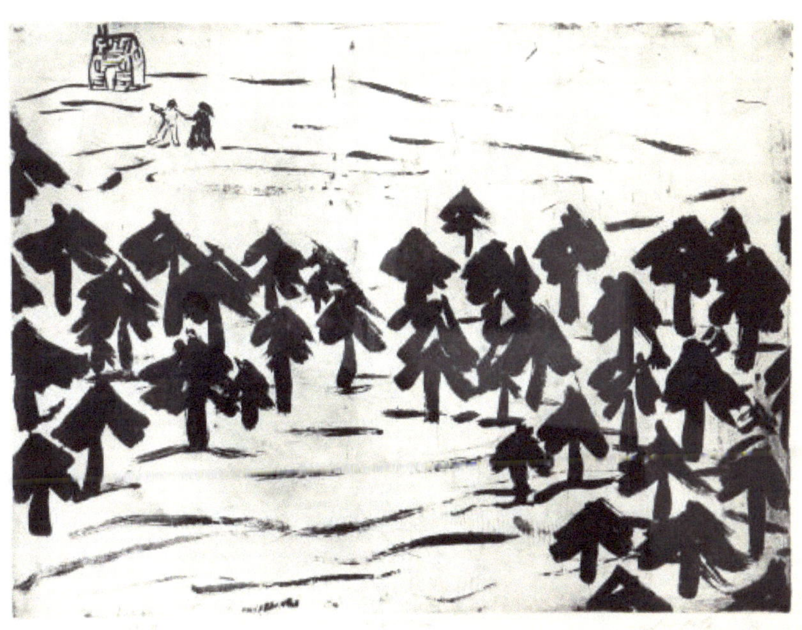

**Plate 7**
Wonsook Kim
*To Our House,* 1976
Lithograph on paper, 17.5 x 23.8 inches
Collection: Artist

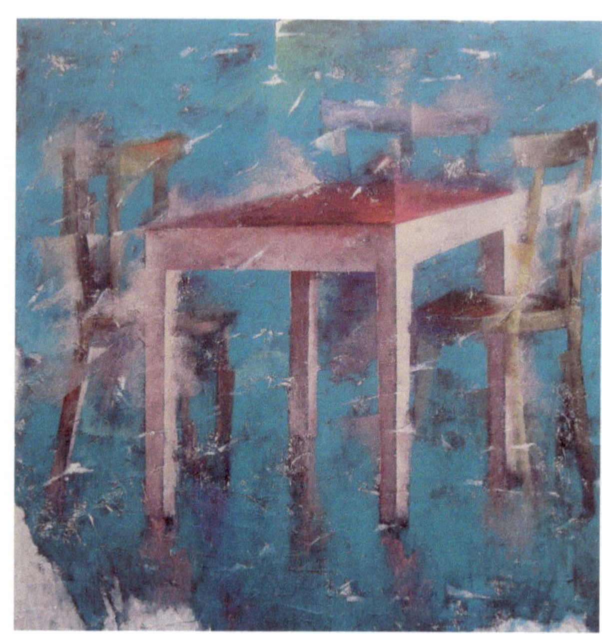

**Plate 8**
Yuran Lee
*Whispering Wood #1*, 1998
Acrylic on canvas, 36 x 36 inches
Collection: Artist

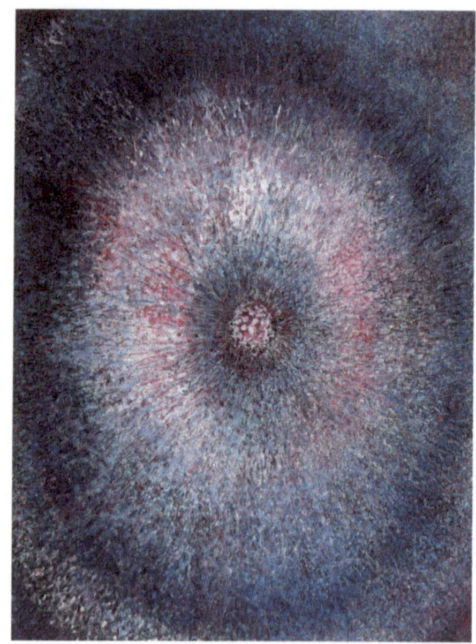

**Plate 9**
Dorothy Deon (Ok Ji Kim)
*Oneness*, 2000 .
Mixed media on plastic, 36 x 36 inches
Collection: Artist

# TRANSPLANTED: KOREAN ARTISTS IN NEW YORK 1955–1989

Kyunghee Pyun

## Theme 1 Going Abstract 1950s–1960s

Many Korean artists who arrived in the United States in the 1950s and 1960s were part of abstract art movements. From around 1958, the Contemporary Artists Association (Hyeondae Misulga Hyeophoe) in Korea was one of the avant-garde art groups that contributed much to the development of the Korean Art *Informel* movement. Its members included Kim Tchang-yeul, Ha In-du, Kim Seo-bong, Cho Yong-ik, Park Seo-bo (b. 1931), Yi Yang-ro, Yi Su-heon and others, Tchang-yeul Kim (b. 1929) came to New York and studied at the Art Students League in 1966–1968, and then went to Paris, encouraged by Nam June Paik. Most of the Association members were born in the 1930s and actively exhibited works in the 1960s.

But before these younger artists came of age, Po Kim and Whanki Kim had been pioneers in finding a voice in abstract art. Both artists were born in 1913 and maintained their friendship in New York in the 1960s, until Whanki Kim's premature death. Po Kim (Bo-hyun Kim is his original name) studied at the Pacific Art School in Tokyo, and returned to Korea in 1946 to start up the fine arts department at Chosun University in Kwangju, Korea. After an agonizing experience during a civilian unrest in the late 1940s, he accepted an invitation from the University of Illinois as a fellow and arrived finally in 1955. Two years later he came to New York City. *(Fig. 16)* He said it was a "shocking" experience to find that American art was being swept up in the frenzy of abstract art at the time of his arrival. As noted by Saleeby-Mulligan in her essay, abstract expressionism was well established by 1955. The premature death of Jackson Pollock in 1956 and the 1958 touring exhibition in Europe, *The New American Painting*, organized by the Museum of Modern Art heightened the canonical status of abstract expressionism.

Whanki Kim went to Paris in 1955, and stayed there for three years. He came to New York in 1963, after having represented Korea in the San Paolo Biennale in 1963. By that time, he was becoming more aware of the international scope of contemporary art. His abstract works during his New York period are often referred to as "Pointillism" or "blue dots." Whanki Kim and his wife became the center the Korean art community in New York *(Fig. 15)*. Many younger artists paid visits to him. After his premature death, Hyang-an Kim set up the Whanki Foundation and opened the Whanki Museum in Seoul in 1992.

In the 1950s during a closer alliance between Korea and the United States at the time of the Cold War, Korean artists made direct contact with American modern art. In 1956, works of American college students were

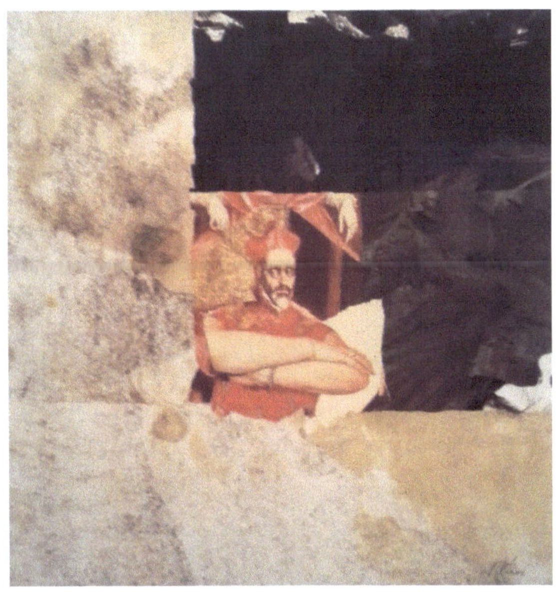

**Figure 16.**
Po Kim. *Small Collage 12*, 1979-1980. Mixed media, 12 x 12 inches. Collection: Artist

shown at Seoul National University. The following year, *Eight American Artists,* an exhibit featuring Mark Tobey, Morris Graves, Kenneth Callahan, Guy Anderson, David Hare, Seymour Lipton, Ergio Mattaeri, and Rhys Kapparn was held at the National Museum of Korea in Deoksugung Palace. More Korean students began applying for

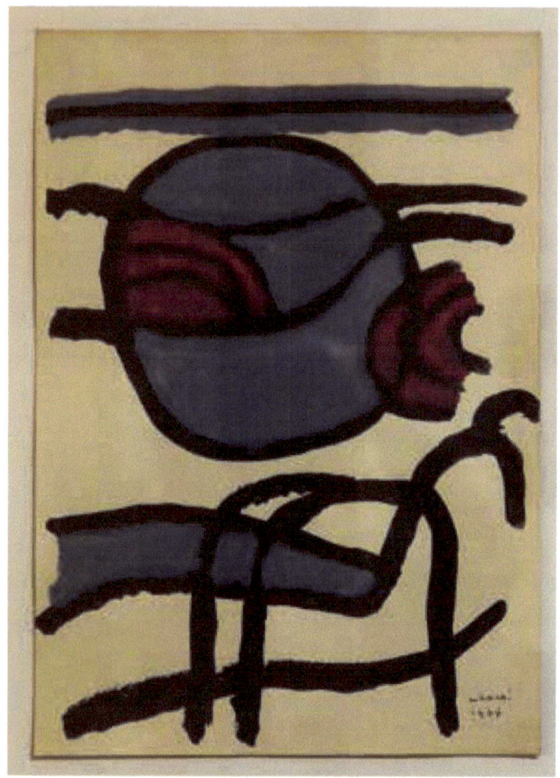

**Figure 15.**
Whanki Kim. *Mountain and Moon,* 1964. Gouache on paper, 11.75 x 8.5 inches.
Collection: Ms. Sook Nyu Lee Kim

American exchange or fellowship programs at higher education institutions to study in MFA programs.

A group of artists who usually studied at the College of Fine Arts at Seoul National University instead headed for New York in the 1960s. Yong Jin Han (b. 1934) and his wife, Moon Mi-aie (1937–2004), and Byoung Ok Min (b. 1941) all arrived in the early 1960s to study in MFA programs. Mi-aie Moon went to the Seoul High School of Music and Art and then studied at the Hopkin Center in Dartmouth College. Yong Jin Han presented his works at the San Paolo Biennale in 1963 and then came to the United States. *(Plate 3).* Both Han and Moon spent a few years in Denmark and France in the 1960s. Han graduated from Columbia University Art School in 1981. The precociously talented young artist, Byoung Ok Min, graduated with an award presented by the President of the Republic of Korea from Seoul National University, and received an MFA degree at Pratt Institute in 1967.*(Plate 2)* She is one of the earliest Korean graduates at Pratt. Moon and Min went to the same high school nd college, and retained their life-long friendship in New York. Like young artists in Korea, these Korean artists created abstract art works. Han was a hard-core sculptor working with iron, bronze, stone, and wood. Bong Tae Kim (b. 1937), a friend of Moon's, went to the Otis Art Institute in Los Angeles and received his BFA and MFA in 1966. Myeung Ro Youn (b. 1936) was in New York in the 1960s and went to Pratt Graphics Center in New York in 1970 while Sungja Moon (b. 1945) studied at the School of the Museum of Fine Arts in Boston in 1967–70[1]. Moon went to art schools in the 1980s.

In the late 1950s and the 1960s, many American artists were inspired by Marcel Duchamp and Dada; some of these artists, John Cage, Jasper Johns, and Robert Rauschenberg, were discovered by the notable art dealer Leo Castelli, who had an Upper East Side gallery. John Cage in turn met Korean artist Nam June Paik (1932–2006) in 1956, and this led to Paik's became part of the Fluxus artists group in New York in the 1960s with George Maciunas, Yoko Ono, and George Brecht.

Johns and Rauschenberg became quite prominent because of the exhibition *The Art of Assemblage* held in 1961 at the Museum of Modern Art. Nonetheless, the mainstream art world of the 1960s still favored "post-painterly abstraction" by such artists as Helen Frankenthaler, Morris Louis, and Kenneth Noland. At the same time, the geometric abstractions of the minimalist painters and sculptors of the late 1950s and early 1960s, artists such as Ad Reinhardt, Donald Judd, and Frank Stella, continued to be influential and were shown at the Green Gallery, Pace Gallery, and Leo Castelli Gallery. In the early 1960s, Andy Warhol's pop art and the comic book-inspired images of Roy Lichtenstein drew attention.

But Korean artists who arrived in the 1960s stayed within the mainstream of "post-painterly abstraction"

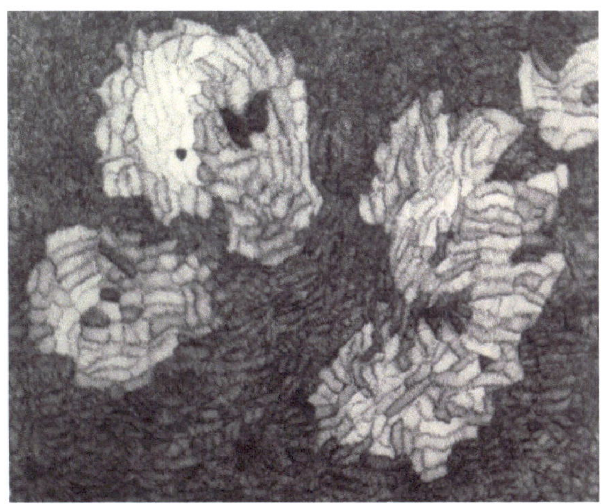

**Figure 17.**
John Pai, *Untitled*, 1985. Print, 30 x 24 inches. Collection Ms. Eun Young Kang

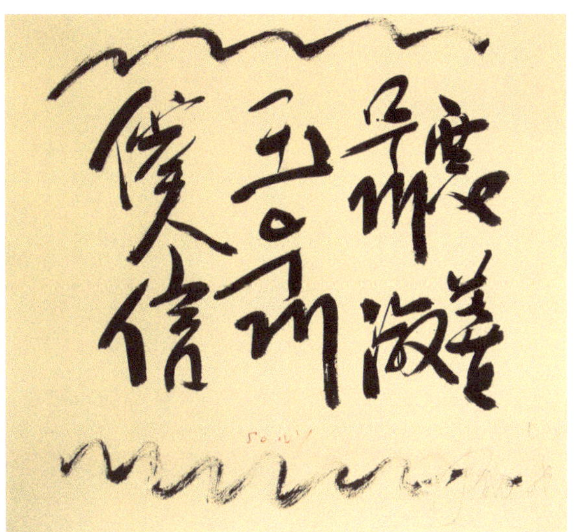

**Figure 18.**
Nam June Paik. *Untitled*, 1989. Ink on paper, 17. 8 x 19.5 inches. Collection: Mrs. Sook Nyu Lee Kim

and "geometric minimalism." While most of these Korean artists were struggling to be known on the New York art scene through school and gallery contacts, Nam June Paik and John Pai (b. 1937) were already prominent in the 1960s. *(Fig. 17)* Nam June Paik, having studied history of art and music at the University of Tokyo, was studying music in Germany when he was introduced to the Fluxus Group by John Cage. In 1965 Paik had his first solo exhibition, *Electronic Art*, at Galeria Bonino, New York. *(Fig. 18)* John Pai, a Korean-American sculptor, earned admiration for his minimalist sculpture inspiring images of nature; he also became chairman of the undergrad sculpture program at Pratt Institute in 1965–1974.

An exhibition entitled Asian *Traditions/Modern Expressions: Asian American Artists and Abstraction, 1945–1970* organized in 1990 by Michael Wechsler, curator of the Jane Voorhees Zimmerli Art Museum at the State University of New Jersey, Rutgers, showed abstract art works inspired by Asian traditions in the 1960s. Whanki Kim, Po Kim, John Pai, and Nong (Robert Han) were included along with Soojai Lee (b. 1933), Byungki Kim (b. 1936), Sung-woo Chun (b. 1934), and Dongkuk Ahn (b. 1937 ; known as Don). Kim, Chun, and Ahn either studied or taught at the College of Fine Arts, Seoul National University; Lee studied and taught at Ewha Women's University. Ahn studied for his MFA at Pratt Institute in 1962–1965. Kim came to New York representing Korea as commissioner at the 1965 San Paolo Biennale and layer taught at Skidmore College and Empire State College in New York. Lee and Chun returned to Korea after completing their degrees in the 1960s.

During this period the activities of Korean and Korean-American artists at galleries and art institutions were somewhat selective and limited. Most of these artists had more shows in the 1970s, after their academic training or perhaps following their adjustment to their new environment.

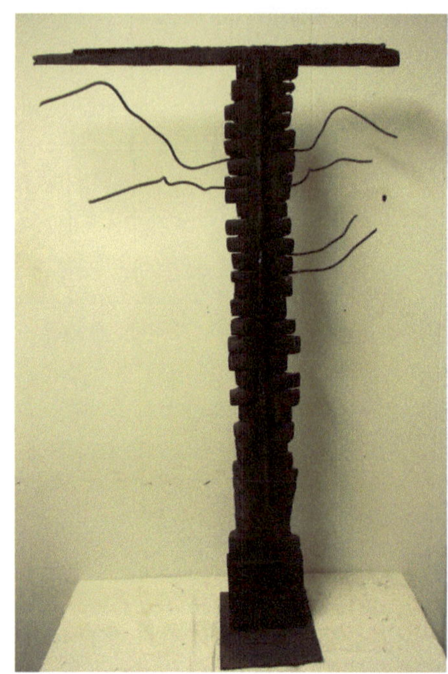

**Plate 10**
Chong Yun Kim
*Untitled,* 1985
Wood and metal, 32 x 10 x 46 inches
Collection: Artist

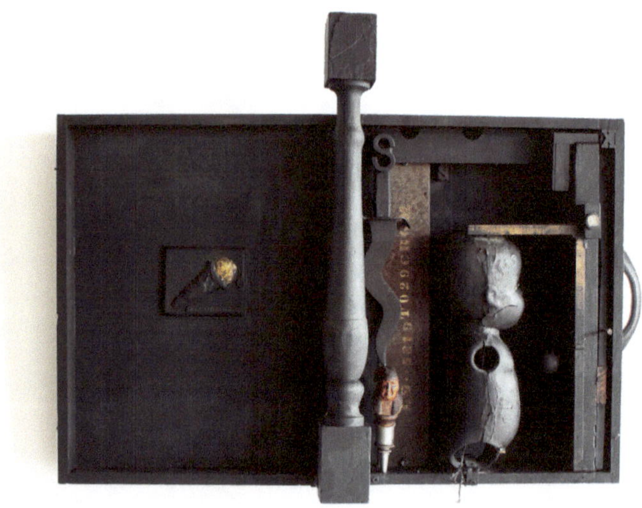

**Plate 11**
Chong Gon Byun
*Gold Ice Cream,* 1982
Mixed media, 24.5 x 32 x 6 inches
Collection: Artist

## THEME 2 BECOMING CEREBRAL 1970s

According to Saleeby-Mulligan's essay in this catalogue, the 1970s was a turbulent time resulting in the coexistence of established styles of abstract and minimalist art along with the emergence of several new styles, including, conceptual art, earth art, and body art (which was often informed by feminist art practice). It is notable that more and more art works or projects became public oriented or socially engaged. Like the political climate of this period, as represented by the civil rights movement, women's rights, and the anti-Vietnam War movements, the artwork of this time was often confrontational, and reflected animosity toward the art market system. Some artists focused on creative work that was either nonobjective or too cumbersome to be included in the gallery system.

This spirit of anti-establishment was favorable to Korean or Korean-American artists. Those who arrived in the 1960s were more visible in gallery space, and young artists also found an audience. The monochrome art movement in Korea from the 1970s to the early 1980s was the Korean response to America's minimalism and Japan's Moho-ha tradition. Seo-bo Park, who was a leader of the *Informel* from the end of 1950s, became an outstanding advocate for monochrome art in the early 1970s.

Korean artists who came here in the 1970s also reflected more diverse styles. At one end, there is an artist like Eel-dan Choi (b. 1937), a graduate of the College of Fine Arts at Seoul National University, who went to Paris to study traditional Korean ink painting with Ungno Lee and then settled in New York. *(Fig. 21)* At another end, we have Choong Sup Lim (b. 1941), also a graduate of Seoul National University, who went abroad somewhat late in life for professional accomplishment, and discovered mixed-media painting and installation.*(Plate 4)* Lim arrived here in 1973 as a recipient of the Max Beckmann Memorial Scholarship at the Brooklyn Museum Art School. He received his MFA at New York University in 1993 while Choi studied at the Central Academy of Art in Beijing in the 1980s. *(Fig. 19 and 20)*

Between these extreme cases are many young artists who came here for MFA programs. Among them are some artists notable in the medium of printmaking, such as Tchah-sup Kim (b. 1940) who came to Pratt in 1974 to study printmaking and painting.*(Fig 22 and 23)* In the beginning his printmaking received much attention

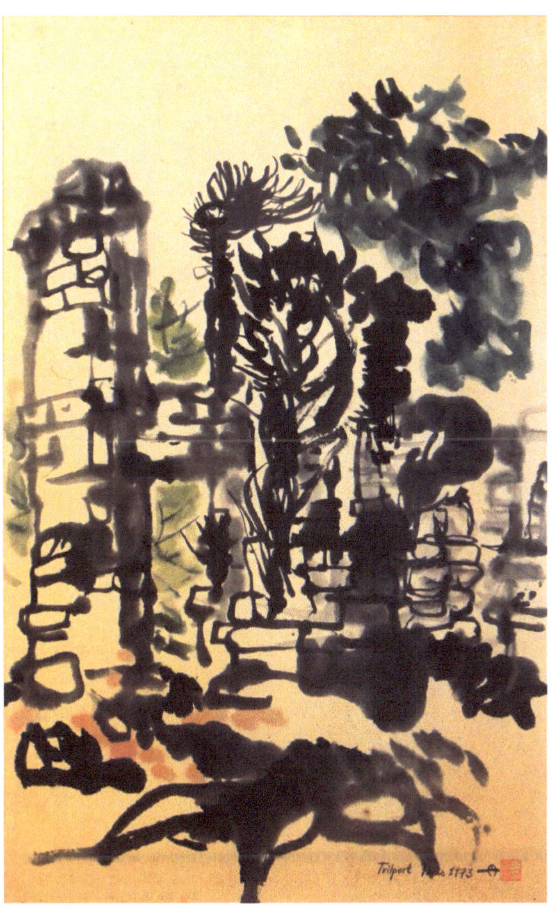

**Figure 21.**
Elaine Il Dan Choi. *Trilport* (outside Paris), 1973. Ink and color on paper, 40 x 28 inches. Collection: Artist

*(Plate 5);* he gained recognition through the acquisition of his printed work by the Museum of Modern Art in 1976 *(Triangle between Infinites,* etching; acc. 219.1976), and in 1995 an oil painting was acquired by the Metropolitan Museum of Art (Hand, Oil on printed paper glued to canvas; acc. 1995.517.6). A print by Kyu-baik Hwang (b. 1932) was also purchased by the Museum

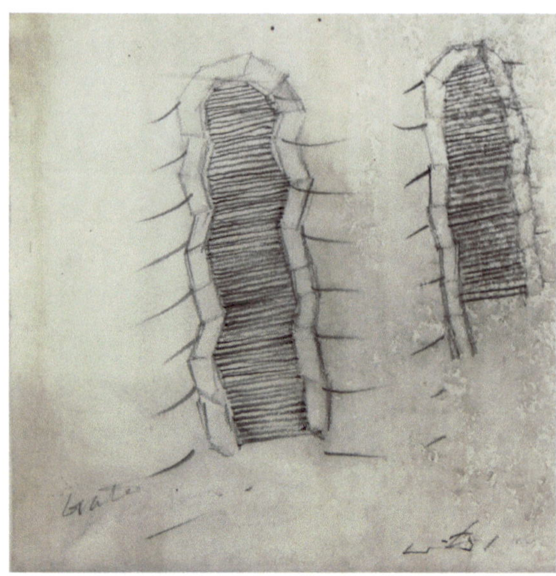

**Figure 19.**
Choong Sup Lim.
*Drawing,* 1995. Pencil on paper, 6 x 11 3/8 inches. Collection: Artist

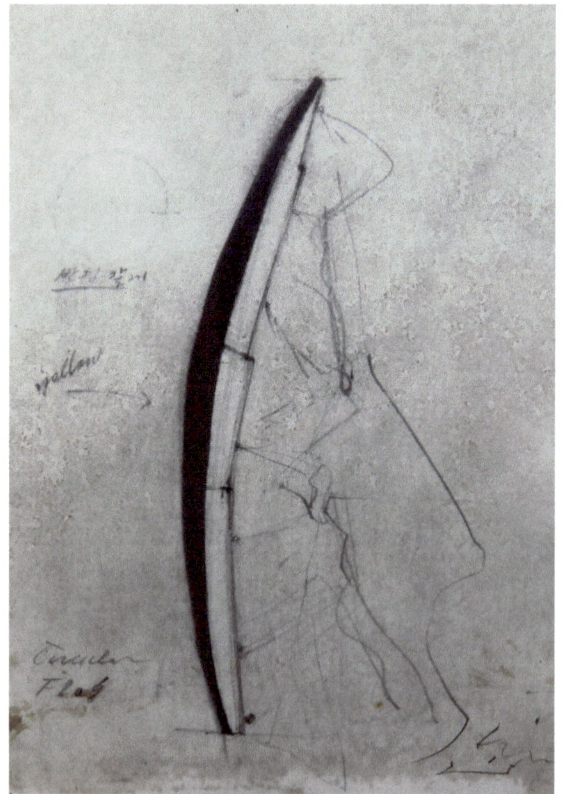


**Figure 20.**
Choong Sup Lim.
*Drawing,* 1995. Pencil on paper, 8 3/8 x 12 inches. Collection: Artist

of Modern Art in 1973 (White Handkerchief on the Grass, Etching and roulette; acc 323.1973); the Museum of Fine Arts in Boston had acquired Escorte De La Voix Lactéé earlier in 1970 (acc. 1970.564). Hwang went to Paris in 1968 to study art history at the Ecole du Louvre and printmaking at the celebrated Atelier 17 under Stanley Hayter. He settled in New York in 1970. He presented color mezzotint works of familiar objects in a surrealist setting with subtle colors at the Print Club, Philadelphia (1971, 73, 75) and at the Miami Graphic Biennale held at the Miami Art Center in 1973. *(Fig 24)*

Woong Kim (b. 1944) came to the United States in 1970 and studied at the School of Visual Arts until 1976 and then at Yale University until 1978. He taught at the School of Visual Arts from 1979–1987. Continuing the tradition of abstract painting, he experimented with thick impasto, collage, and cutout *(Plate 6)* fabrics. In 1976 his large wall painting entitled *Korean Mural* was acquired as part of a public art commission by the City of Roanoke to be displayed at the Roanoke Performing Arts Center in Virginia. This was an important accomplishment for the community of Korean-American artists. With public art being more prevalent in the 1980s, more Korean-American artists were able to win civic commissions in places like New York and increase their exposure to the mainstream media as well. Woong Kim, Choi, and Han showed variations of abstract painting instilled with traditions of Korean art. Boon-ja Choi (b. 1952) came to study at Columbus College of Art and Design in Ohio in 1975–77, and continued her work at the Art Institute of Philadelphia in 1978–80 *(Fig. 25);* her husband at the time, Kyu-nam Han (b. 1945), received his MFA at the Ohio State University in 1977. As co-curator, Han also organized a significant group exhibition at Sarah Lawrence College in 1982, highlighting the unique aesthetics of abstract painting by leading Korean-American artists. *(Fig. 26)*

A younger artist among those arriving in the 1970s is Wonsook Kim (b. 1953). During her BFA program at Hong-ik University, she had an opportunity to come to the United States in 1972 and study at the University of Illinois for a BFA and MFA. Her figurative paintings of women, birds, flowers, and landscapes in color and black ink stimulate a viewer's nostalgia and sympathy in a mood of surrealism reminiscent of Frida Kahlo or Marc Chagall.*(Plate 7)*. Though she was not an outspoken feminist artist, she was a pioneer in focusing on the experience of women and their social roles as mother, lover, sister, dreamer, and so on.

In the 1980s and 1990s more Korean-American artists grappled with this kind of personal journey as the main subject of their work beyond formal exploration of geometric minimalism and abstract art. After settling in San Francisco in 1970s, Youn Hee Paik

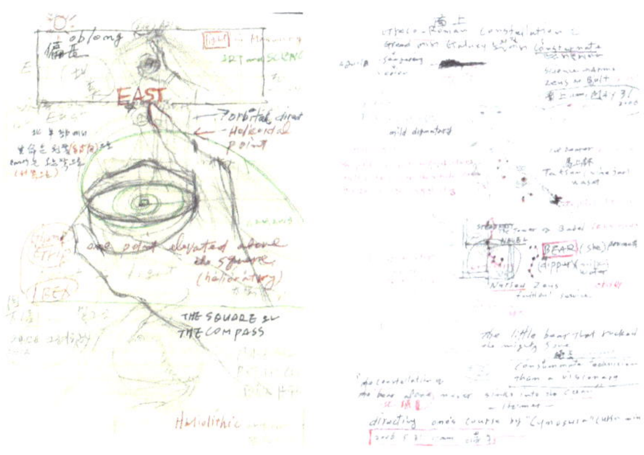

**Figure 22.** **Figure 23.**

**Figure 22.**
Tchah Sup Kim. *Drawing of Art & Science*, 2013. Pencil and pen on paper, 5 7/8 x 8 5/8 inches. Collection: Artist

**Figure 23.**
Tchah Sup Kim. *Self Portrait*, 2006. Pencil and pen on paper, 7 1/4 x 9 5/8 inches. Collection: Artist

(b. 1945) exhibited her expansive visions of the nostalgic universe at the Wingluk Memorial Museum in Seattle, Washington (1984), the San Bernadino County Museum in San Bernadino, California (1985), and the Jose Museum of Art in San Jose, California (1986). Having attended Seoul High School of Arts and Seoul National University, she knew Mi-aie Moon, Yong-jin Han, Byoungki Kim, and Byoung-ok Min, along with many other expatriate artists. She currently has studios in New York and San Francisco. Su Kwak (b. 1949) arrived in the United States in 1973, and earned her undergraduate degree at the University of St. Thomas in Houston, Texas. She then studied at the University of Chicago for her MFA. Like Paik, Kwak also paints views of the sky, usually with the sun or other natural elements. In the early

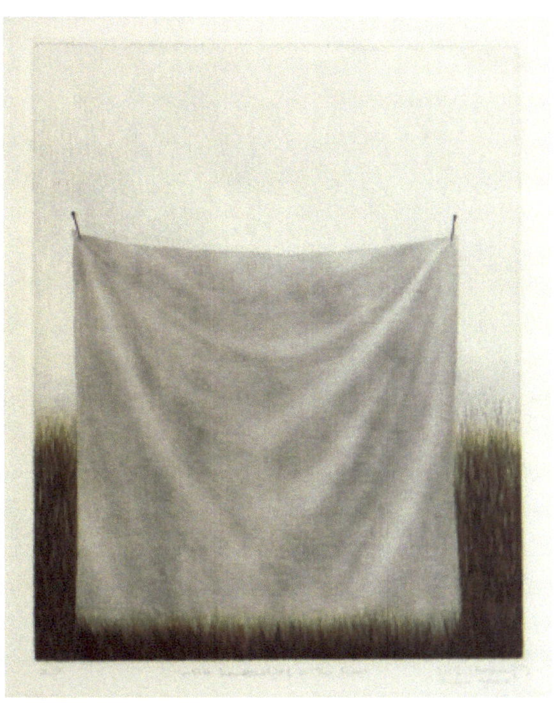

**Figure 24.**
Kyu Back Hwang. *Handkerchief*, 1979 (?). Print, 24 x 16 inches. Collection: Mrs. Sook Nyu Lee Kim

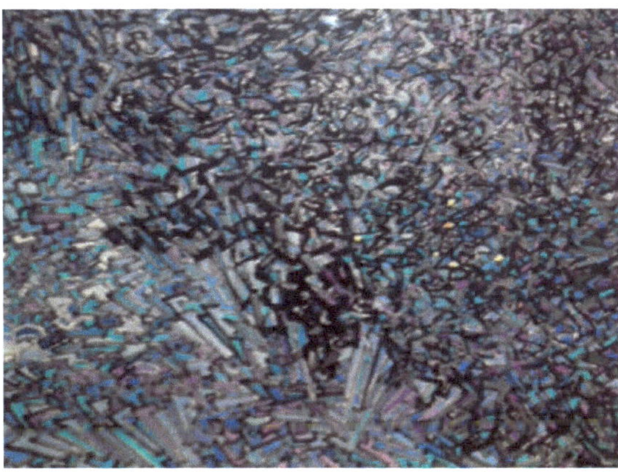

**Figure 25.**
Boon Ja Choi. [Title unknown], 1982 (?). Water color on rice paper, 47 x 32 inches. Collection: Ms. Eun Young Kang

1980s, she exhibited at the Queens Museum of Art and the Henry Street Settlement in New York. She is currently working in the Washington DC area.

Yuran Lee and Dorothy Deon (aka Ok-ji Kim) also arrived in the 1970s to pursue careers in art. Deon went to the Fashion Institute of Technology and then studied at the Art Students League in New York *(Palte 9)*. Deon briefly ran Han Kook Gallery in 1982–84. Chong Yun Kim (b. 1949), a son of Byoungki Kim, graduated from Hong-ik University, and then came to New York to study at Pratt Institute where he majored in sculpture.*(Plate 10)*. Along with Yong-jin Han, he uses stone, wood, and metal.*(Fig. 28)*

Kwang Young Chun (b. 1944) studied at Philadelphia College of Art and showed his work at commercial galleries in New York, Philadelphia, and in the Delaware area in the 1970s. Soo-cheon Jheon (b. 1947) came from Japan to study at Pratt in the late 1970s. Unlike other Korean-American artists, Chun and Jheon decided to go back to Korea while exhibiting their work at international art shows and galleries. They based their studio in Seoul, and became outstanding artists with global exposure. For example, Chun had several solo exhibitions at art galleries and public institutions in the United States and Japan; Jheon represented Korea at the 54th Venice Biennale in 1995 and Sao Paolo Biennale in 1996.

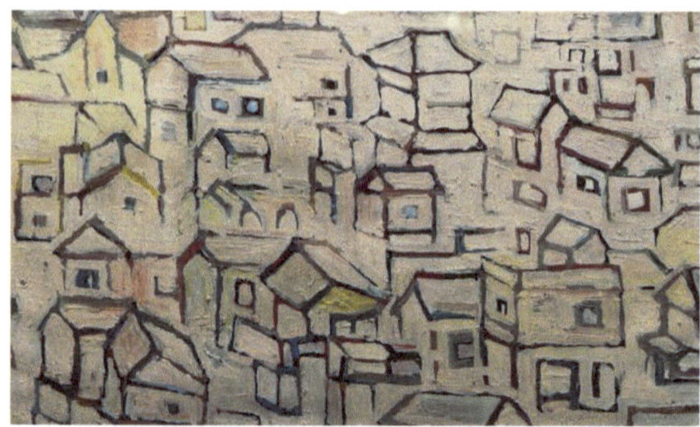

**Figure 26.**
Kyu Nam Han. *Untitled,* 1980s (?). Oil on canvas, 37 x 27 inches. Collection: Ms. Eun Young Kang

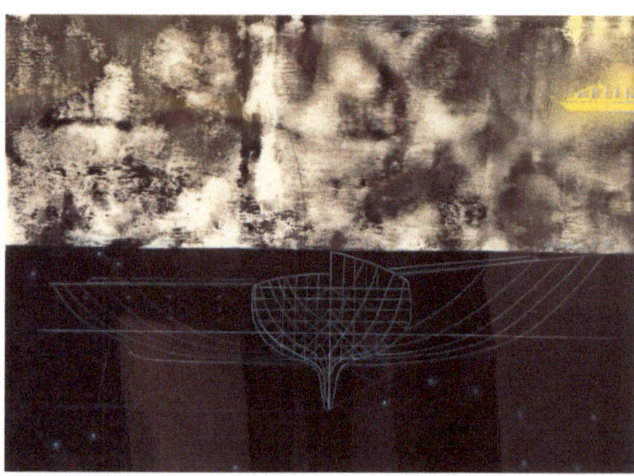

**Figure 27.**
Youn Hee Paik. *Ship-West,* 1997. Acrylic on paper, 30 x 42 inches. Collection: Artist

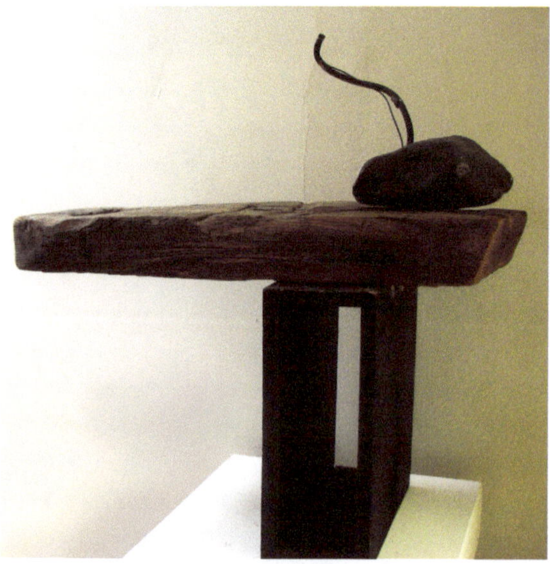

**Figure 28.**
Chong Yun Kim. *Untitled,* 1980. Stone, wood, and metal, 30 x 13 x 30 inches. Collection: Artist

## THEME 3 UNIQUE, UNIQUE, UNIQUE 1980s

Numerous art students from Korea arrived in this country in the 1980s to work on their MFA degrees. Many returned to Korea, but many others remained and settled here. For those young artists, Nam-June Paik was a great inspiration. The Whitney Museum of American Art mounted a major retrospective of Paik's works in 1982. In 1984 and 1986, via satellite, Paik launched a project instantly broadcast around the world. A major American artist, he was a central figure among Korean-American artists as well.

In the Korean-American art community, which was dominated by painters, usually inclined to the tradition of intelligent and serene abstract art, several younger artists came up with unique ideas. Mikyung Kim (b. 1956), who received her MFA at Pratt in 1983 showed a series of ambitious conceptual art works in the form of sculpture. Using wood, glass, steel, rubber, oil and mixed media, her works resemble a minimalist installation.*(Plate 12)* On the other hand, these are not cold and rigid representations of objects. In her mind they are related to her biographical experiences. Another Korean artist who suddenly showed up in New York in 1980s transformed moments of his life into art works. Originally from Daegu, Chong Gon Byun (b. 1948) studied at the Art Students League in 1981–84. *(Plate 11).* Unlike younger artists who came to earn MFA degrees, he was already well known in Korea as the grand-prix winner of the Dong A Art Festival / Visual Art Competition hosted by *Dong-A Ilbo (Dong-A Daily Newspaper)* in its inaugural year 1978. At the time, there was tight censorship of newspapers by the Korean government, which also cast a suspicious look at Byun, whose work depicting an American military base seemed to send an anti-government message. Byun's hyper-realism began a new trend among young artists and proved to be quite popular in the United States. He had many solo exhibitions at the Riverdale Gallery in the 1980s, and was later honored with successful shows at public art institutions in Korea. Upon settling in Harlem, he started to create assemblage works combining found objects with his own realistic painting, reminiscent of works of Marcel Duchamp and Robert Rauschenberg but more painstaking and sophisticated *(Fig. 7)*. His works and exhibitions also drew the attention of mainstream art critics, and he was reviewed in the New York Times. Both Mikyung Kim and Chong Gon Byun signaled formation of diverse styles among Korean-American artists in the late 1980s and the 1990s.

Daru-Jung Hyang Kim (b. 1955) arrived in 1977 with a BFA from Seoul National University; she received her MFA at Pratt in 1980. Her landscape-inspiring abstract dots and circles followed the tradition of abstract painting with more optimistic and jovial tones *(Plate 14)*. She now develops these paintings into larger formats for public art projects. Ill Lee (b. 1952) went to Hong-ik University and came to study at Pratt in 1978. He developed his famous ballpoint pen paintings on a large canvas in the 1980s. Myong Hi Kim (b. 1949), wife of Tchah-Sup Kim came to New York in 1976 to work on her MFA at Pratt. *(Plate 13)*. Having studied at Seoul National University and earned both a BFA and MFA, she was well known in Korea. Unlike other Korea artists pursuing the tradition of abstract painting, she presented more realistic painting on a chalkboard.

A return to the figurative style was prevalent in art scenes of New York in the 1980s as well. Soo Im Lee (b. 1954), wife of Il Lee arrived in the 1980s, after having obtained a BFA and MFA in painting from Hong-ik University. *(Plate 15 and 16)*. She studied printmaking at New York University, graduating with a master's degree. In the 1990s she was represented by Art Projects International, which was founded in 1993 by Jung Lee Sanders, a Korean-American art dealer. Two couples, Myong Hi Kim and Tchah-Sup Kim; Il Lee and Soo Im Lee were fortunate to have the privilege of belonging to a professional art gallery.*(Plate 17)*

Sung Hee Cho, who graduated from Hong-ik University

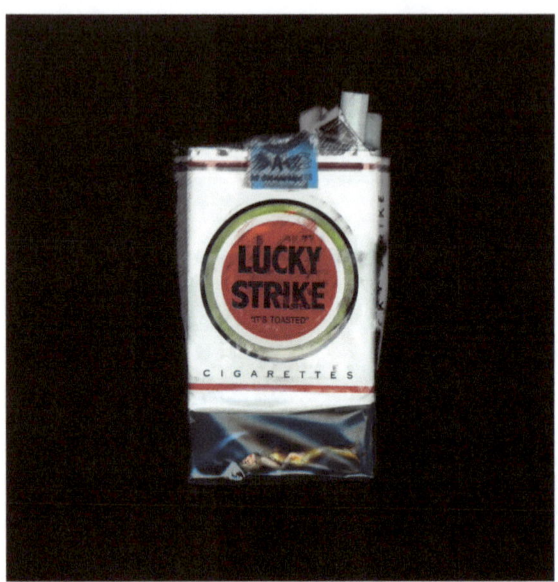


**Figure 29.**
Won Jun Park. *Lucky Strike with Marilyn Monroe*, 1989. Digital photography, 11 x 8.5 inches. Collection: Artist

in 1972, came to New York in the late 1970s, and studied at Parsons School of Design and Pratt in the early 1980s. *(Plate 18)* Among Korean artists, there were also some who chose photography as a major medium. Jinhong Kim and Wonjun Park discovered photography as fine art after they arrived in the United States. Jinhong Kim graduated from Memphis College of Art and Pratt *(Plate 20)* ; Wonjun Park came in 1973 and took classes at the International Center of Photography while holding down many jobs in order to support his family.*(Plate 19)*. Kim runs his own photo studio in Fort Lee, New Jersey, whereas Park ran a one-hour photo shop near Times Square until he died of cancer in 2009. Park took photos of signboards, people, and New York streets, and edited with special effects. It is moving to know that he edited and reworked his photography up to the last moments of his life.

Yeong Gill Kim (b. 1957) came to New York in the late 1980s and worked on intricately woven layers of images often referred to as Zen, Daoism, or Eastern philosophy. Sometimes more abstract, other times more figurative like an old photograph, Kim tactfully hides his versatile techniques and multi-step work processes on a serene and sentimental canvas *(Fig. 30 and 31)*. On the other hand, a painter like Sang Nam Lee (b. 1953) incorporated a universal form of graphic art in his work. He earned his BFA from Hong-ik University in 1978 and moved to New York in 1981. He paints in a color-field style but with graphic touches. His colors are more vibrant than the minimalist art of the 1960s.

Seong Lee (b. 1960) obtained a BFA in drawing from Maryland Institute College of Art in Baltimore and an MFA in painting at Pratt in the 1980s. *(Fig. 32)* Primarily working with materials discovered on the street or in other surroundings such as wood scraps, dishes tree roots, broken TVs, VCRs, and bottles, he creates assemblage works, both large installations as well, as portable works. He is also an art professor at Long Island University.

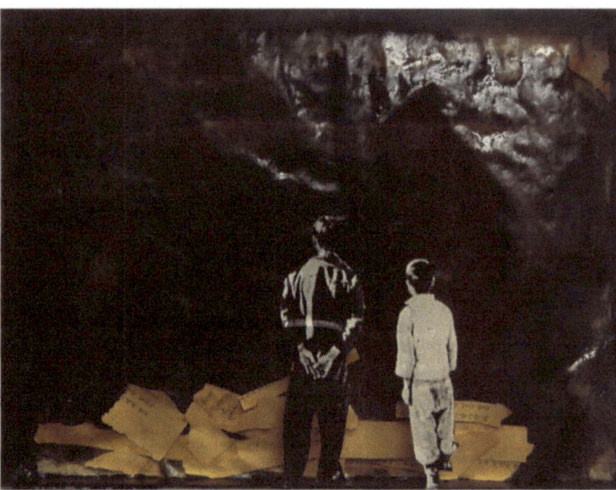

**Figure 30.**
Yeong Gill Kim. *Old Box*, 1991. Mixed media, 10 x 12 inches. Collection: Artist

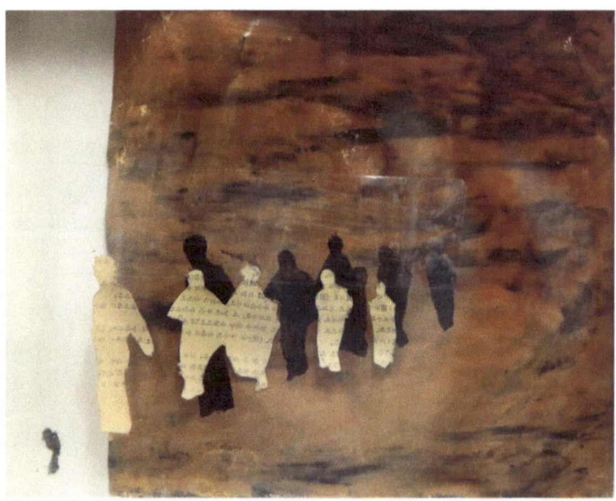

**Figure 31.**
Yeong Gill Kim. *Father and Son*, 1991. Mixed Media, 10 x 12 inches. Collection: Artist

While Seung Lee is remembered as an artist of bottles, Eung Ho Park is often known as the "sperm spoon" artist. After studying at Portland State University in 1980–82, he earned his BFA at Pratt in 1984.

In-kie Whang (b. 1951) was originally an engineering major at Seoul National University but changed to fine arts and graduated in 1975. He completed his MFA at Pratt in 1981, and actively participated in group exhibitions until the mid-1980s. He then went back to Korea to teach at Sunkyunkwan University. His painting, *Village* was acquired by the Metropolitan Museum of Art in 1995 (Village, 1991, Bronze paint with metal on canvas; acc 1995.517.1). In 2003 he represented Korea at the Venice Biennale along with Yiso Bahc.

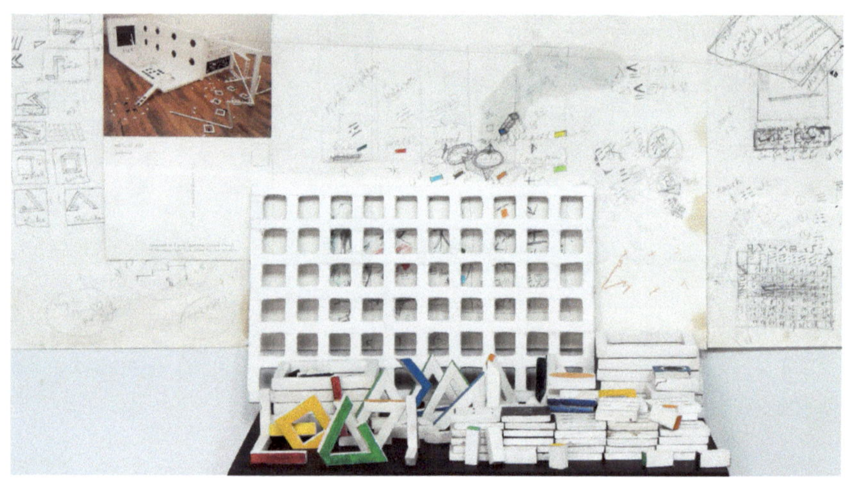

**Plate 12**
Mi Kyung Kim
Idea scathes, parts from *Untitled 64*, 1983
Acrylic on wood, 50 x 24 x 14 inches
Collection: Artist

(Original Installation)
*Untitled 64*, 1983
Acrylic on wood, 8 x 2 x 5 feet

## THEME 4 SEARCH FOR AN IDENTITY 1980s

In the 1980s a group of young artists were searching for their identity. In Korea, Minjung art had some impact and was introduced to Korea-American artists in exhibitions such as *Minjoong Art: A New Cultural Movement from Korea* in 1988; it was organized by Wan Kyung Sung and Hyuk Um with an exhibition and video programs at the Artists Space. A related panel discussion included Hal Foster and Lucy Lippard, well-known art critics, along with two curators.

More artists began to create films or performances as part of their visual art works, and some Korean-American artists who grew up in the anti-Vietnam War climate and protest culture also reconnected with Korean artists working in the United States. Sung-ho Choi (b. 1954) was one of those young artists deeply interested in socially meaningful art projects. He arrived in 1981 to study at Pratt after studying at Hong-ik University, and settled in the New York community of Korean artists. Thinking of the isolated and individual artists of the 1960s and 1970s, Choi saw the necessity as well as the opportunity to organize an artist community. He eventually founded Seoro Korean Cultural Network in the 1990s with his friends, and initiated a large-scale exhibition of Korean-American artists called *Across the Pacific: Contemporary Korean and Korean-American Art* at Queens Museum of Art in 1993 *(Fig. 10,11 and 13)*. He worked with mixed media, combining the heritage of Korea and his adopted country, America *(Plate 23)*. His works, such as *American Pie*(1996), became public art projects in the 1990s. His earlier installation with photographs, plants, wood, lighting fixtures, *Choi's Market* (1993) showing a family photograph of parents and two children inside a grocery is a touching testimony to the huge migration of Korean people looking for a land of opportunity in the 1980s.

Choi's friend, Mo Bahc (Yiso Bahc) (1957–2004) also went to Hong-ik University and then Pratt. In 1981 Bahc immigrated to New York with his family and lived here for fifteen years, returning to Korea in 1995. Like Choi, he pursued more socially charged art works; he ran Minor Injury, an alternative art gallery for minority artists, in Brooklyn until 1989. Like other conceptual artists in the 1980s, he made installations using found objects and ready-made images along with famous advertisement phrases from anti-Communist posters or commercial art. With the growing attention he received in Korea and abroad, he represented Korea in the 2003 Venice Biennale. *(Fig. 11: handwriting of Yiso Park)*

Y. David Chung, was born in Bonn, Germany, and educated in the United States, earning a BFA from the University of Virginia's Corcoran College of Art and Design in 1988 and an MFA from George Mason University in 2002. He is currently a professor at the School of Art & Design at the University of Michigan. As a multimedia artist and filmmaker known for his film and video work, installations, drawings, prints, and public artworks, he created many works in which he discussed his identity as a Korean-American man. In 1992 Turtle Boat Head was commissioned by Thelma Golden for the Whitney Museum of American Art. On panels of white walls, images of Korean life, past and present, from the Japanese Occupation to urban America were drawn in bold charcoal black.

Byron Kim (b. 1961) immigrated to America as a child. He received a BA from Yale University in 1983, and then attended Skowhegan School of Painting and Sculpture. Many younger Korean artists would later earn residency there. He has been exhibiting in solo and two-person shows since 1992 and has exhibited with artists such as Kiki Smith and Glenn Ligon. He was reviewed in the *New York Times, Artforum, NY Arts, New Yorker, Washington Post, Art in America, Newsweek, Los Angeles Times, and the Washington Post;* he is currently represented by Max Protetch. Mr. Kim was appointed senior critic in painting/print making at the Yale University School of Art in 2009.

He was selected for the Whitney Biennial in 1993 Biennial Exhibition at Whitney Museum of American Art, New York. *Synecdoche* (1991–present), first included in the 1993 Biennial, is a continuing project of portraiture now comprising more than 400 panels, each a single hue ranging from light tan or pink to dark brown; it was acquired by the National Gallery of Art in Washington DC in 2009.

Joseph Pang (b. 1965), who immigrated as a teenager in 1981, was honored in 1983 with the New York City Young Artist Award organized by the Metropolitan Museum of Art. After briefly attending the Art Students League, in 1985, he went to the State University of New York at Stony Brook and received a BA in studio art and philosophy in 1987. He received an MA in painting and philosophy from Yale University in 1991. In the 1980s he was a minister and did not exhibit his works in public until 2005. But he continued his creative journey and made abstract paintings and figurative paintings in mixed media on canvas *(Plate 24)*.

After studying at Hong-ik University and participating in the Paris Biennale in 1960, Chan Seung Jung (1942–1994) finally came to New York in 1980. . He had the unique position in Korean art history of being a performance artist. He settled in New York, with a studio in Brooklyn, and befriended younger artists from Korea. He also frequented Mo Bahc's Minor Injury gallery.

Theresa Hakyung Cha (1951–1982) was a novelist and performance artist, who came to American with her family in 1962. They lived in Hawaii and then California. She earned her BA and MA in Comparative Literature and studied with Jim Melchert to earn her MFA from the University of California, Berkeley. After college she spent time in Paris studying filmmaking and critical theory with Christian Metz, Raymond Bellour, and Thierry Kuntzel in 1976. It was a tragedy that Cha was brutally murdered in New York City one week after the publication of her novel, *Dictee*[2]. Her novel, *Dictee*, includes photographs, diagrams, and stories in the voices of various women: the Korean revolutionary Yu Guan Soon, Joan of Arc, Hyung Soon Huo (Cha's mother, who was born in Manchuria to first-generation Korean exiles), Demeter, Persephone, and Cha herself. Her presence as a Korean-American performing artist in New York created renewed interest in "Korean-ness" as an immigrant artist among art critics in the early 1980s.[3]

After graduating from Hong-ik University, Ik-Joong Kang (b. 1960) arrived in New York to get his MFA at Pratt in 1984. Working with tiny paintings and assembling them on a large scale, he worked with many subjects taken from Korean traditions *(Plate. 25)*. Like other Korean artists in the 1980s he exerted much effort in discovering who he was and how he should employ his cultural heritage. His solo exhibition at the Whitney Museum of American Art at Philip Morris, New York in 1996 was a triumphant moment following in the footsteps of Nam June Paik, Y. David Chung, and Byron Kim. In 1997 he was awarded the Special Merit prize in the 47th Venice Biennale.

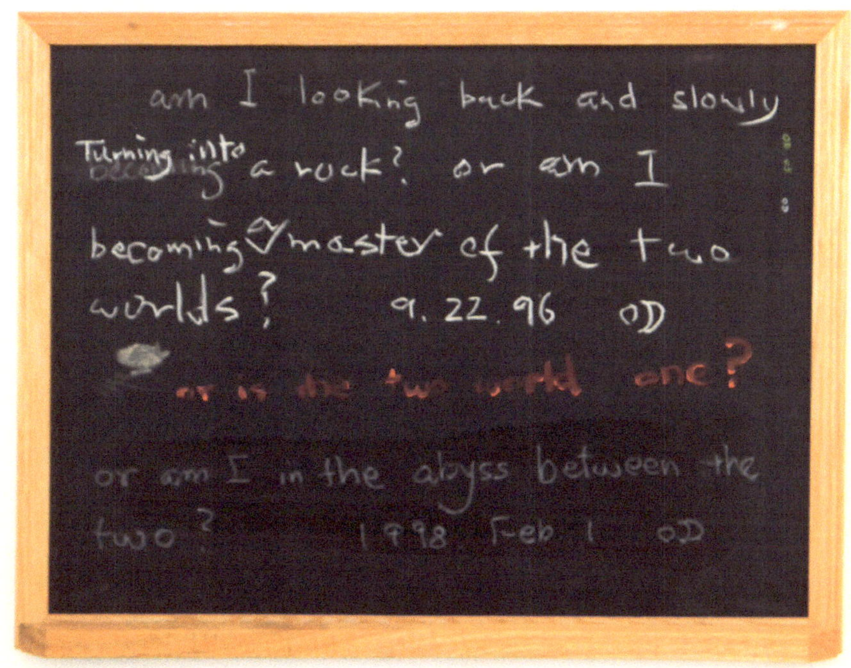


**Plate 13**
Myong Hi Kim
*Master of the Two Worlds,* 1996-1998
Oil-pastel on chalkboard, 18 x 24 inches
Collection: Artist

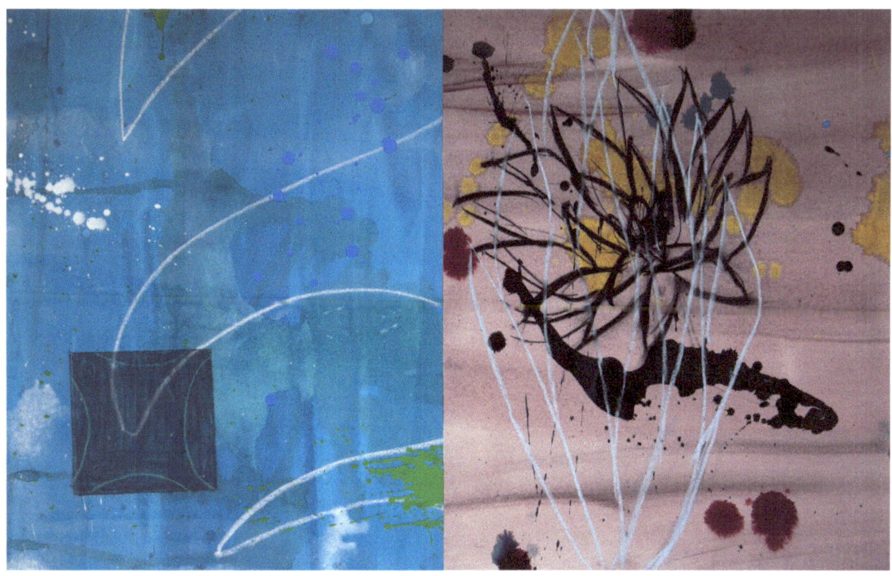

**Plate 14**
Daru-Jung hyang Kim
*Lotus,* 1995
Mixed Medium on paper, 24 x 32 inches
Collection: Artist

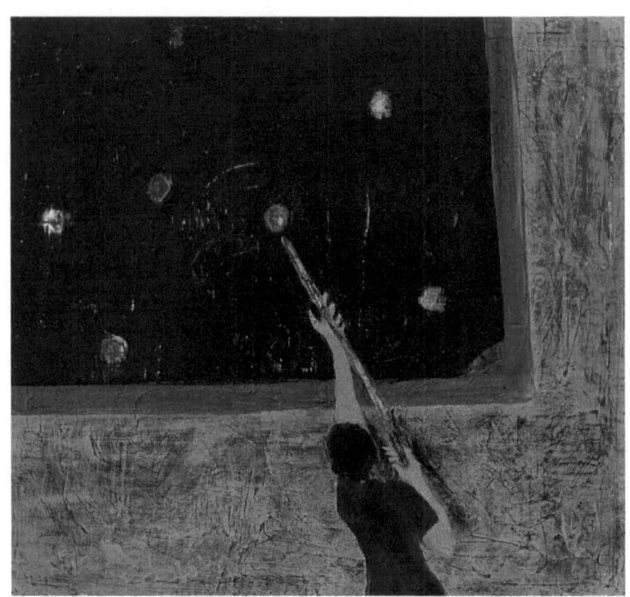

**Plate 15**
Soo Im Lee
*Pink Ball,* 1998
Acrylic on woodblock, 12 x 11 inches
Collection: Artist

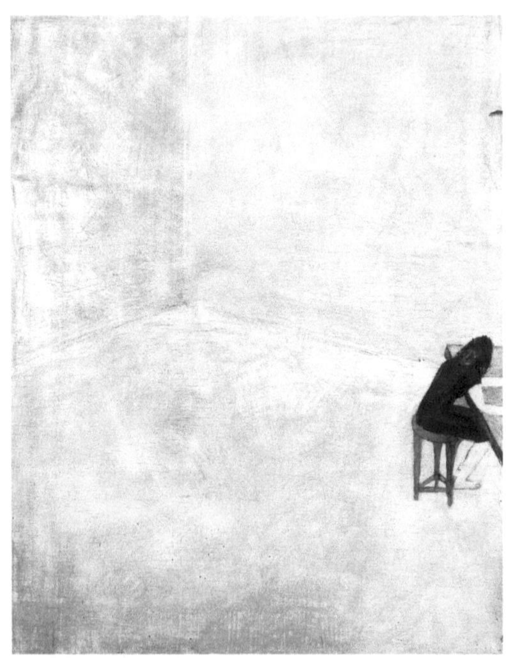

**Plate 16**
Soo Im Lee
*Freeman at Corner,* 2002
Acrylic on woodblock, 20 x 16 inches
Collection: Artist

## THEME 5 LOOKING AHEAD FOR THE NEXT CENTURY

Korean artists who arrived in the late 1980s will be included in the second part of the exhibition of the Archive of Korean American Artists. Because they were studying until the end of the 1980s, their activities in the 1990s were partially included in this exhibition. A major trend in the 1990s was interest in public art or audience-engaged art. Even artists who arrived in the 1970s would present new installations at this time. Choong Sup Lim is a good example. Youn Hee Paik also created a new format of installation by hanging or arranging her large canvas cloths in gallery space.

Sook Jin Jo (b. 1960), who received an MFA at Hong-ik University in 1985, came to New York and earned a second MFA at Pratt in 1991. It was remarkable that she had her first solo exhibition at the historically famous O. K. Harris Works of Art in 1990. Its founder, Ivan C. Karp (1926–2012) was an art critic for the *Village Voice* in the 1950s and promoted the early careers of pop artists as a co-director of the Leo Castelli Gallery from 1959 to 1969. O. K. Harris Works of Art opened in 1969 and became one of first galleries to promote the Photo Realist Movement and exhibit the work of Duane Hanson, Deborah Butterfield, Manny Farber, Richard Pettibone, Robert Cottingham, Marilyn Levine, Nancy Rubins, Luis Jiminez, Jack Goldstein, Al Souza and many others. Subsequently she appeared in a documentary video featuring thirteen artists, including Jenny Holzer, Ilya Kavakov, Cindy Sherman, and Jennifer Bartlett. Many art critics such as Donald Kuspit, Eleanor Heartney, and Robert Morgan wrote about her work. Perhaps inspired by earth art or environmental art of the 1970s, Jo discovers old, used, and abandoned materials that would discovers old, used, and abandoned materials that would have disappeared in time. Although she works mainly with wood, she has created drawings, collages, and photography along with her famous sculptural assemblages, performances and site-specific installations.

Jungjin Lee (b. 1961) studied ceramics at Hong-ik University and came to New York in the late 1980s to earn her MFA in photography at New York University in 1991. Some of her works from a series called *American Desert* in 1993 and 1994 were acquired and given to the Metropolitan Museum of Art; her work has been exhibited in Los Angeles and Europe as well. Theresa Chong (b. 1965) received her BFA from Boston University School of Fine Arts in 1989 and an MFA from the School of Visual Arts in 1991. Having studied cello at Oberlin College, she came under the influence of John Cage. Chong's works of dots and lines on paper are unique in a sense that her abstract imageries resonate with even more abstract form of music.

Sung Ho Choi, Sook Jin Jo, Daru-Jung Hyang Kim, and In-joong Kan continue to show large-scale works in public space or gallery space. In the late 1990s and the 2000s, the generation born in the 1970s would join them and introduce a wide range of styles such as video art, photography, mixed media, performance, documentary films and other new forms.

## NOTES

1) Several Korean artists still went to Paris. For example, Soohee Shin (b. 1944) and Choong Heum Park (b. 1946) went to Paris after graduating from Seoul National University. Shin studied at the Ecole Nationale Superieure de Beaux-Arts in 1966–68 while Park in 1977–82.

2) She was a victim of a criminal assault in New York City.

3) Amei Wallach, "Theresa Cha: In Death, Lost And Found (Art/Architecture)," April 20, 2003. Her exhibition "A Dream of the Audience" was on view at the Bronx Museum of Arts in 2003.

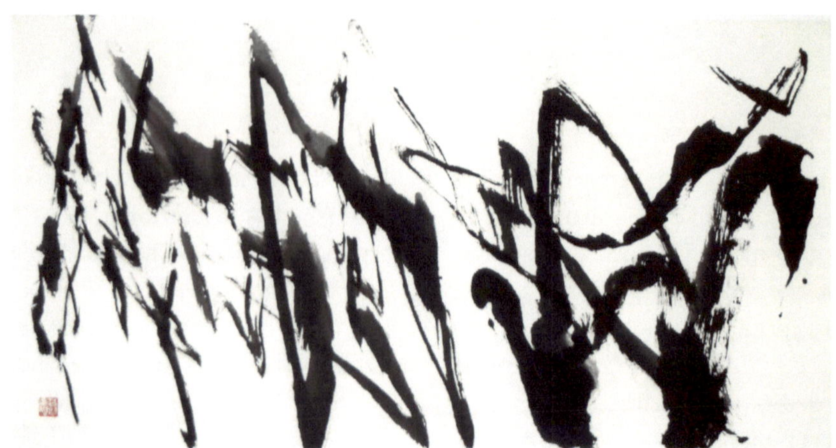

**Plate 17**
Ju Sang Kim
*Strolling*, 2011
Ink on Korean rice paper, 14 x 24 inches
Collection: Artist

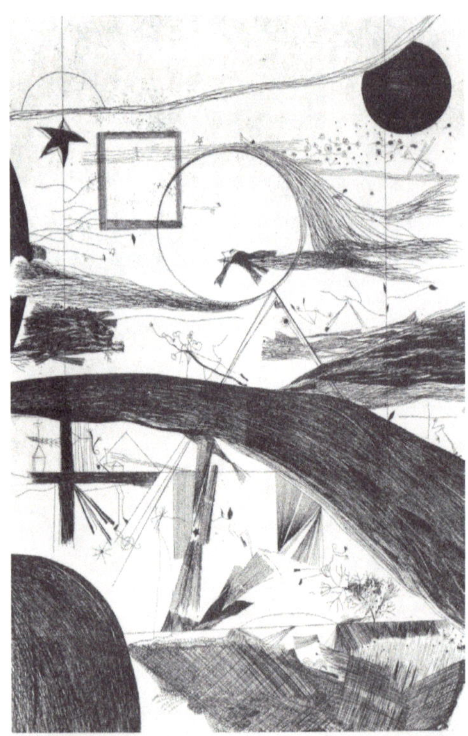


**Plate 18**
Sung Hee Cho
*An Illusion*, 1981
Etching and mezzotint with colors, 37 x 30 inches
Collection: Mrs. Sook Nyu Lee Kim

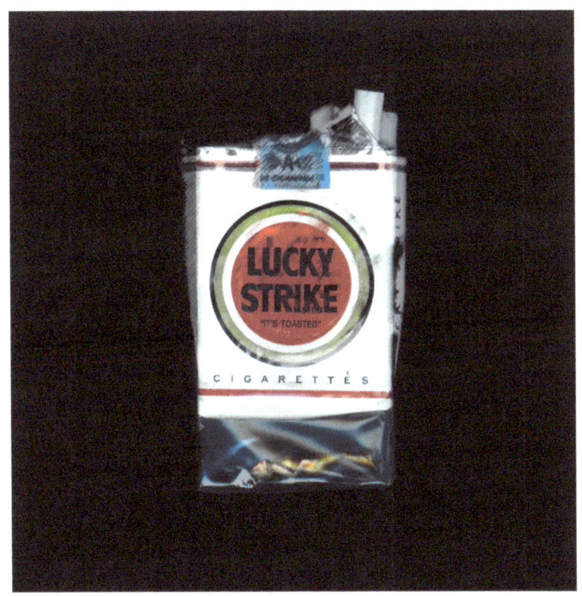


**Plate 19**
Won Jun Park
*It's Me*, 1989
Digital photography 11 x 8.5 inches
Collection: Artist

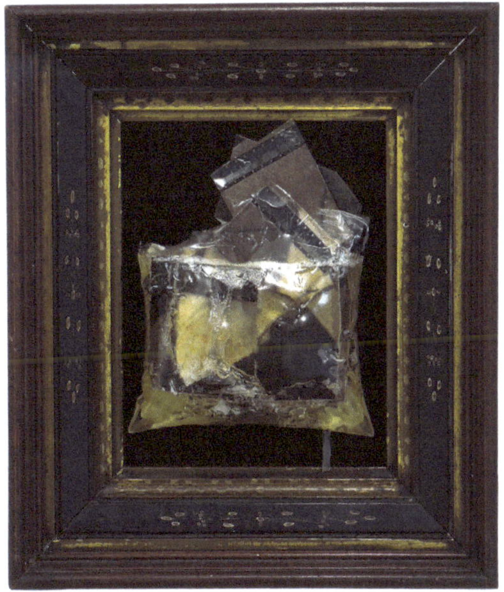

**Plate 21**
Seung Lee
*Film Collaged Drawing in ZipLock Bag*, 1985-2005
Mixed media, 12 x 14 inches
Collection: Artist

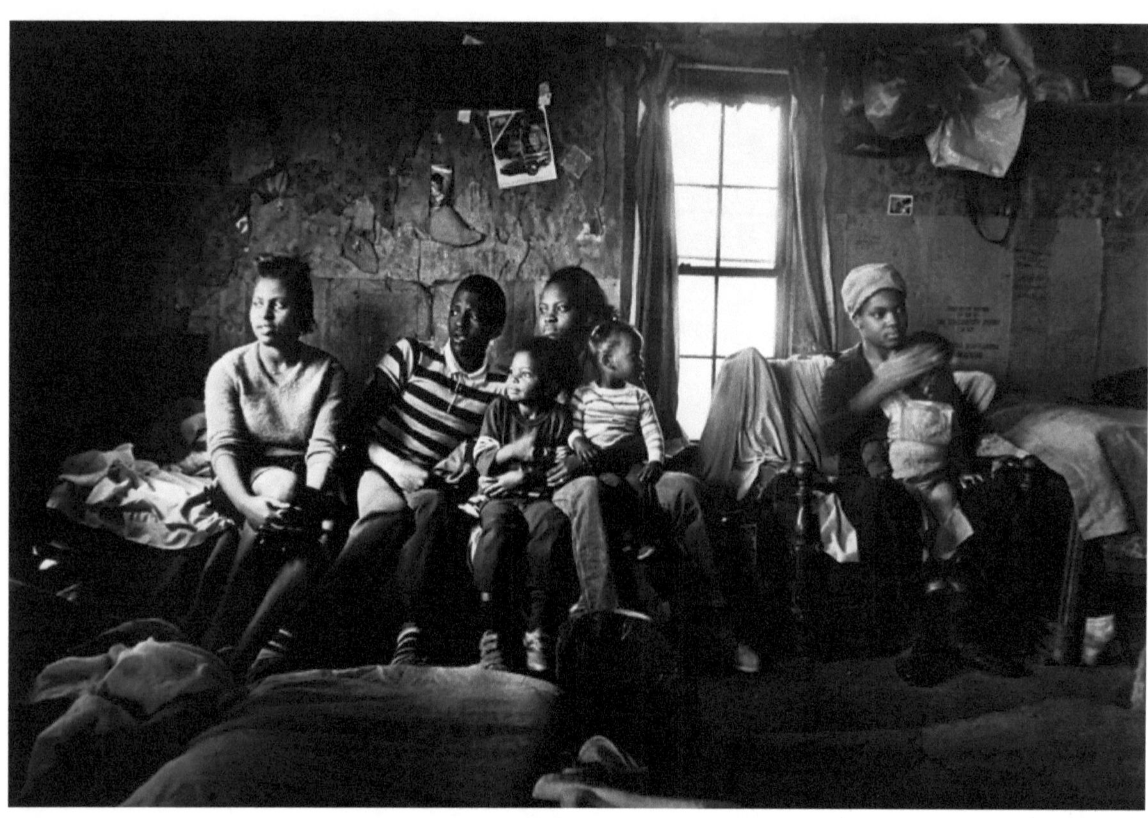

**Plate 20**
Jin Hong Kim
*People*, 1984
Kodak RC paper, 12x17 inches
Collection: Artist

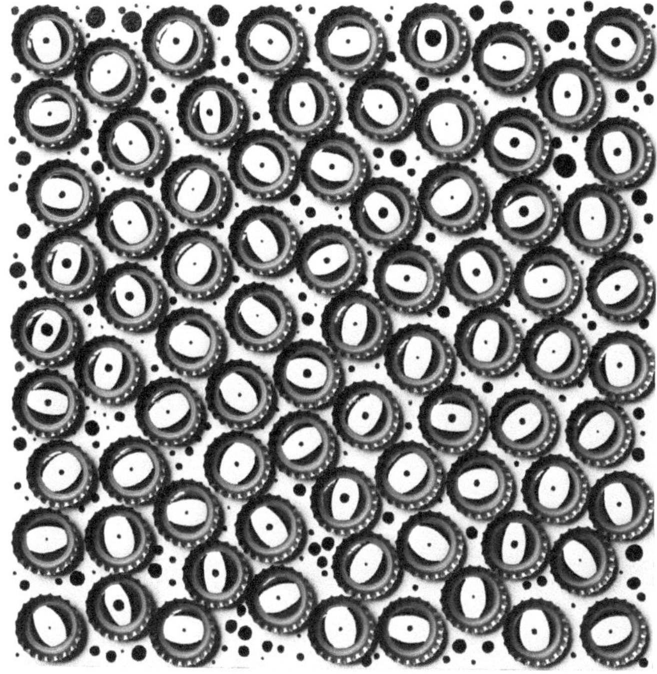

**Plate 22**
Eung Ho Park
*Shocked,* 2012
Epoxy resin, oil and bottle caps on wood, 12 x 12 x 1 inches
Courtesy of Y Gallery

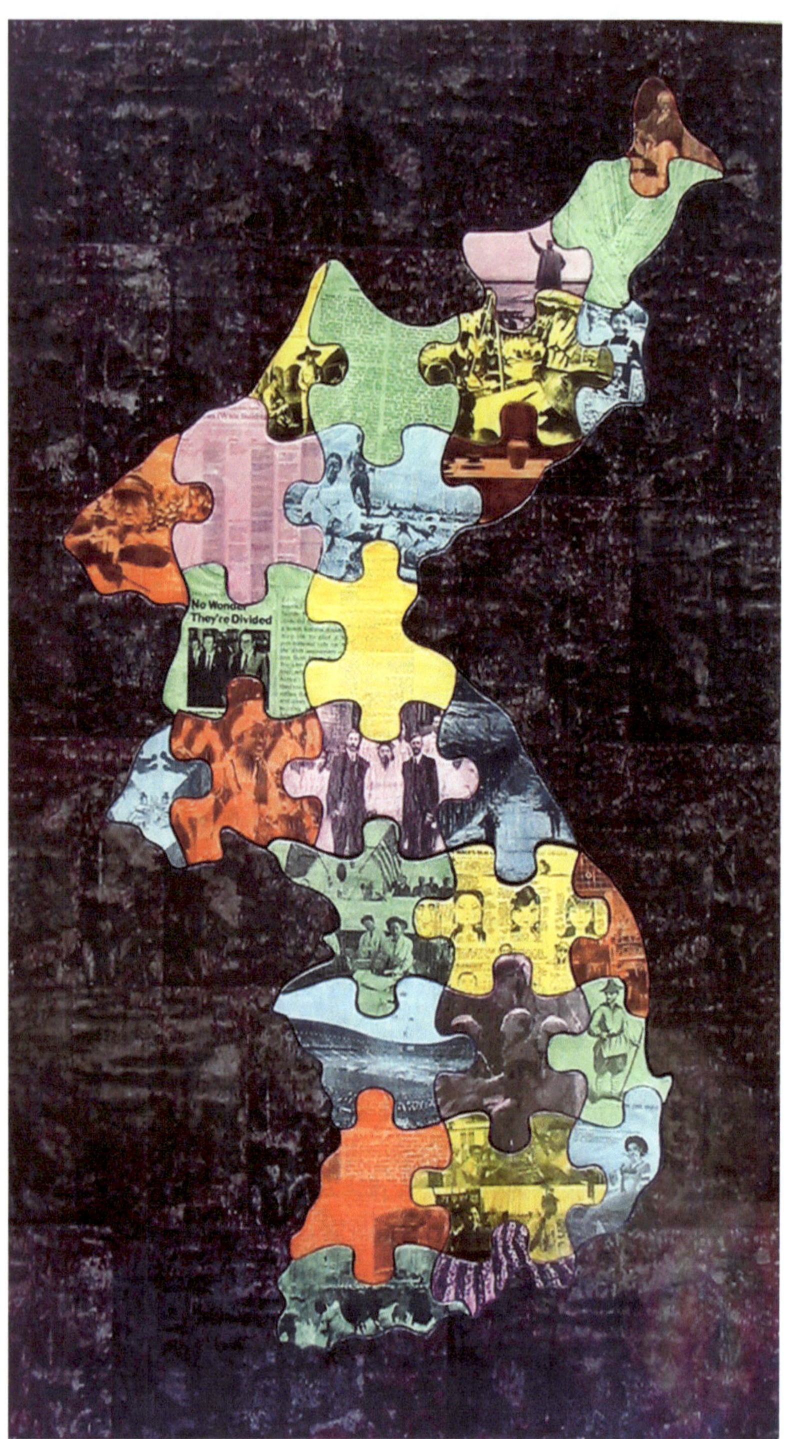


**Plate 23**
Sung Ho Choi
*Their Korea*, 1994
Mixed media on wood, 84 x 48 inches
Collection: Artist

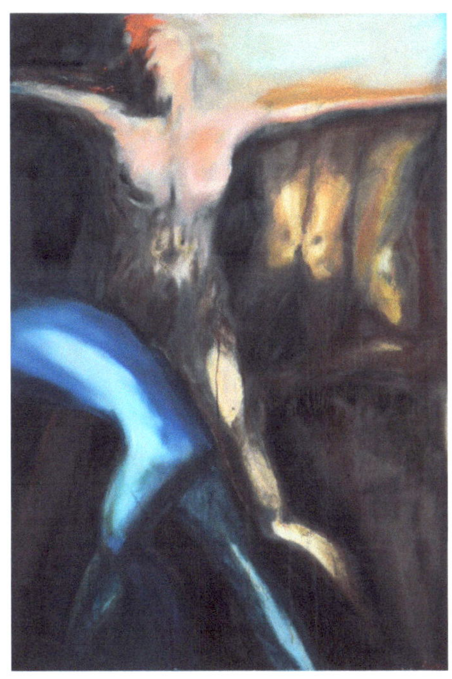

**Plate 24**
Joseph Pang
*Epiphany in Passion*, 1987
Oil on canvas, 39 x 56 Inches
Collection: Artist

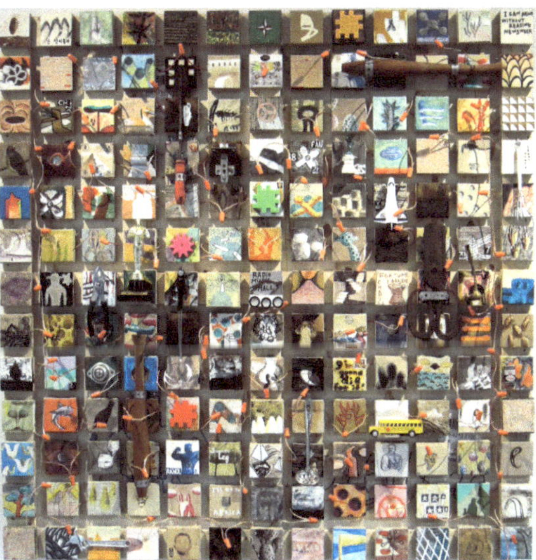

**Plate 25**
Ik-Joong Kang .
*Happy World,* 1984-1990
Mixed media on wood, 51 x 51 inches.
Collection: Artist

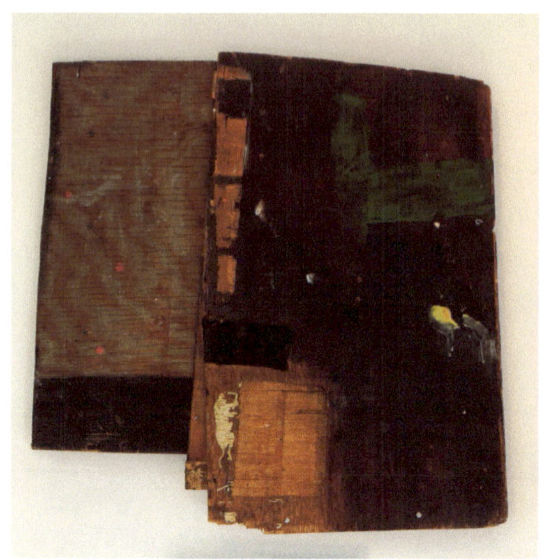

**Plate 26**
Sook Jin Jo
*Untitled*, 2002
Oil on plywood, 2.5 x 29 x 3 inches
Collection: Artist

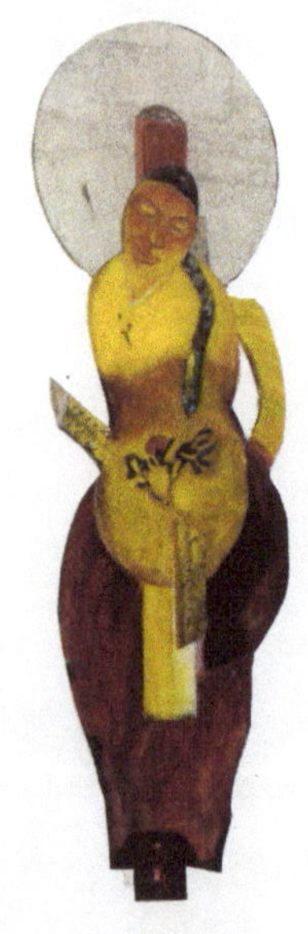

**Plate 27.**
Sunny Hyun Sook Soe
*The Mother*, 1996.
Oil on wood, flexi glass, 8.5 x 3 feet .
Collection: Artist

# APPENDIX 1: SELECTED EXHIBITIONS 1950's–1980's

## SELECTED EXHIBITIONS IN THE 1950's

1951 "Korea: The Impact of War in Photographs," Museum of Modern Art

1958 "Contemporary Korean Paintings," World HouseGalleries

1958 Obelisk Gallery, Washington DC (Soojai Lee)

## SELECTED EXHIBITIONS IN THE 1960's

1962 Korea Art Exhibition at Seattle World's Fair (Dongkuk Ahn or Don Ahn)

1962 Kornblee Gallery, New York (Po Kim)

1963 7th Sao Paolo Bienal (Yong Jin Han; Whanki Kim)

1965 8th Sao Paolo Bienal (Byungki Kim; Tchang-yeul Kim)

1965 E. B. Crocker Art Gallery, Sacramento (Nong or Robert Han)Santa Barbara Museum of Art (Nongor Robert Han)

1967 Georgia Museum of Art, University of Georgia, Athens(Nong or Robert Han)

1968 Vincent Price Gallery, Chicago (Soojai Lee)

1968 "Contemporary Korean Painting" at the National Museum of Modern Art, Tokyo

1966 Contemporary Artists Group, Aage Damgaard, Denmark (Mi Aie Moon)

1966 Herning Museum, Denmark (Yong Jin Han)

## SELECTED EXHIBITIONS IN THE 1970's

1971 Poindexter Gallery, New York (Whanki Kim)

1972 Holly Solomon Gallery (98 Greene Street Loft at the time), New York (Kwang Young Chun)

1974 New Artists Show, Artists Space, SoHo, New York (Byoung-ok Min)

1975 Aldrich Museum Annual 1975, Aldrich Museum of Contemporary Art, Ridgefield, Connecticut (Byoung-ok Min)

1975 Woodmare Gallery, Philadelphia (Kwang Young Chun) Wanamker Gallery, Philadelphia (Kwang Young Chun)

1976 15 New York Artists, University of Colorado (Byoung-ok Min)

1976 SoHo Center for Visual Artists, SoHo, New York

1977 New Talent in Printmaking, A.A.A. Gallery, New York, New York (Tchah-sup Kim)

1977 Acquisition 1973-1976, Museum of Modern Art, New York, New York (Tchah-sup Kim)

1978 Choi, Boon-Ja/Han, Kyu-Nam Paintings, Han Kook Gallery, New York, New York

1978 The 4th Annual Small Works Competition, Grey Gallery, New York University, New York (Choong Sup Lim)

## SELECTED EXHIBITIONS IN THE 1980's

1980 O.K. Harris Gallery. New York, NY (Choong SupLim: solo)

1981 The First Annual Invitational: Current Korean-American Sensibilities, Korean Cultural Service, New York, NY (Choong Sup Lim and others)

1981 30 Years of American Printmaking, Brooklyn Museum, Brooklyn, New York (Tchah-sup Kim)

1981~82 Korean Drawing Now, Brooklyn Museum, Brooklyn, New York

1982 Traditional Korean Pottery; Contemporary Korean Painting, Sarah Lawrence College Art Gallery, Bronxville, New York

1982 New Dimensions in Clay, Brooklyn Museum, Brooklyn, New York (Mikyung Kim)

1983 P.S.122(Painting Space 122), New York, Two-Person Exhibition (Mikyung Kim and Woong Kim)

1988 "Artist in Marketplace" Bronx Museum of the Arts, Bronx, New York (Mikyung Kim)

1989 " Artist in the Marketplace" Bronx Museum of the Arts, Bronx, NY (Daru: Jung Hyang Kim)

## SELECTED EXHIBITIONS IN THE 1980's

1990 Wood Constructions, O.K. Harris Works of Art, New York, NY (Sook Jin Jo 1990s and 2000s)

1990 Landscape Observed and Imagined, Krasdale Gallery, White Plains and Hunts Point, Bronx, New York (Chong Gon Byun)

1990 "Decade of the Marketplace", The Bronx Museum of the Arts, Bronx, NY (Daru: Jung Hyang Kim)

1990 "Serene Insurrection," Souyun Yi Gallery (Yeong Gill Kim, Young Ok Lee, Kwi Hoon Lee)

1991 24 Korean Artists in New York, Haenah-Kent Gallery, New York

1993 Walter Wickiser Gallery, New York, NY (Ahn Dong Kuk, 1993, 94, 96)

1995 Gallery B.A.I., Brooklyn, NY (Chong Gon Byun)

1997 Space Untitled, New York, NY (Chong Gon Byun)

1999 Kim Foster Gallery, New York (Kwang Young Chun)

# APPENDIX 2: LIST OF PATRONS AND GALLERIES

## SECTION 1: PATRONS OF KOREAN - AMERICAN ARTISTS

**Wolhee Choe** (1937 - 2013) was a professor of English at Polytechnic University and translated many Korean books on poetry, painting, and poetics into English. She is an aunt of a visual artist, U-Ram Choe (b. 1970). While living in New York since 1960s, she befriended Nam June Paik, Po Kim, Whanki Kim and his wife, Hyang-an Kim along with many Korean artists. She was not an art critic, but wrote some essays for several Korean artists.

**Matthew Kim** (b. 1928) was a medical doctor in Port Chester, New York. He and his wife knew many Korean literary figures and artists in Korea and supported Korean artists in New York from the 1950s. He is an important collector of Whanki Kim and donated some works to Whanki Museum in Seoul, Korea. He also wrote a memoir published in Korean.

**Sook Nyu Lee Kim** (b. 1937) was the owner of Han Kook Gallery in the 1970s and is currently president of AHL Foundation which she founded in 2003. She invited many Korean artists to exhibit their works in New York in the 1970s and also organized many shows for Korean-American artists in the late 1970s and early 1980s. She is also an important collector of Korean and Korean-American artists.

**Frederic E. Ossorio** (1919–2005) was a Filipino-American businessman and also an art collector in Greenwich, Connecticut. His family ran Victorias Milling Company, a sugar manufacturing company in the Philippines and Ossorio Securities in the US. Educated at Yale and Harvard, he collected diverse genres of art works. His brother, Alfonso A. Ossorio (1916–1990) was a well-known Filipino-American artist and friend of Jackson Pollock. Another brother, Robert Ossorio (1923–1996) was a dancer and founder of the Manhattan School of Ballet. Frederic Ossorio bought several works by Korean-American artists through Sook Nyu Lee Kim of the Han Kook Gallery.

## SECTION 2: GALLERIES AND MUSEUMS

### *1950s and 1960s*

World House Gallery (Herbert Mayer d. 1991; founded in 1953 and closed in 1968; since 1957 in the Carlyle Hotel on Madison Avenue in New York City): The gallery represented an eclectic group of artists from Austria, France, Finland, Greece, Iceland, Italy, Norway, Spain, and Sweden.

### *1970s*

**Artists Space** (founded in 1972 by Trudie Grace and Irving Sandler): currently at 38 Greene Street New York NY 10013 since 1993

**Henry Street Settlement Arts for Living Center** (founded in 1975; now called Louis Abrons Arts Center): 265 Henry Street New York NY 10002

**Holly Solomon Gallery** (Holly Solomon 1934– 2002; founded in 1975 and closed in 2002; 98 Greene Street Loft, alternative space, 1969–1975): early collector of Pop Art, Nam June Paik; Chun Kwang Young (Archive of American Art)

**Lotus Gallery, New York** (1970s): Ahn Dongkuk (1975, 76, 77), Kwang Young Chun (1975, 79)

**OK Harris Works of Art** (Ivan C. Karp 1926–2012; founded in 1969): 485 West Broadway, then at its present address, 383 West Broadway (Karp's records in Archive of American Art)

**Poindexter Gallery** (Elinor Poindexter 1906–1994; founded in 1955 and closed in 1978): Whanki Kim (1971)

Westbeth Gallery, New York, NY (1960s–present; not for profit): 55 Bethune Street New York NY 10014; Ahn Dongkuk (1977)

### *1980s–1990s*

**Alpine New York Gallery** (closed in 1990(?); now Alpine Design, Inc as an antique shop): 230 Fifth Avenue NY 10001 (27th St)

**Art Projects International** (1993–present: founded by a Korean-American art dealer Jung Lee Sanders): originally on Broome Street and then current location in TriBeCa in 2011

**Brooke Alexander, Inc.** (founded by Brooke and Carolyn Alexander in 1968): in a storefront on East 68th Street; 26 East 78th Street in 1972; 20 West 57th Street in 1975; currently at 59 Wooster Street (Soho) New York since 1985

**Haenah-Kent Gallery, New York** (many Korean artists in the 1990s)

**Hankook Gallery** (founded in 1976 at 1140 Avenue of the Americas, New York, NY 10036; in 1979 the gallery moved to 40 West 57th Street New York): 1976–1981 owned by Sook Nyu Lee Kim and 1982–1984 by Dorothy Deon and Youngja Park

**Kang Collection** (1981–present; founded by Keum Ja Kang): 9 East 82nd Street New York, NY 10028

**Korean Cultural Service** (1979–present; Gallery Korea founded in 1986): 460 Park Avenue

**Minor Injury** ((founded by Mo Bahc and Sam Binkley in 1985): 1073 Manhattan Avenue in Greenpoint in 1985; 273 Grand Street in Williamsburg in 1990

**Phoenix Art** (founded in 1958 at 10th Street; artist co-operative community, not-for-profit organization): 210 11th Avenue at 25th Street New York, NY 10001

**Sigma Gallery** (owned by Sunsook Ahn?): 379 West Broadway New York, NY10012 (Yongjin Han and Nam June Paik, 1995)

**Souyun Yi Gallery** (founded by Ms. Yi in the 1990s): 249 Centre Street New York NY 10013 ((John Pai, Yeong Gill Kim)

**Walter Wickiser Gallery** (founded in 1992; son of Ralph Wickiser, New York, NY (Ahn Dong Kuk, 1993, 94, 96)

**---Significant Public Institutions**

**Asian American Artist Alliance** (founded in 1988; formerly as Alliance for Asian American Arts and Culture in the 1970s–1980s): originally at 339 Lafayette Street New York and moved to 20 Jay Street, Suite 740 Brooklyn, NY 11201

**Asian American Arts Centre** (founded in 1974; art exhibition program begun in 1984): 111 Norfolk Street New York, NY 10002; previously at 26 Bowery, 3rd Floor New York, NY 10013 (Chinatown)

**Asia Society Galleries** (Asia Society founded in 1956; art gallery for contemporary Asian art in the early 1990s)

**Bronx Museum of the Arts** (founded in 1971): originally housed in the Bronx County Courthouse and in 1981 moved to 1040 Grand Concourse, Bronx, New York.

**Brooklyn Museum** (since 1895): 200 Eastern Parkway Brooklyn, New York 11238

**Noguchi Museum** (founded in 1985 by Isamu Noguchi (1904–1988), Japanese-American artist): 9-01 33rd Road (at Vernon Boulevard), Long Island City (Queens), NY 11106

**Queens Museum of Art** (founded in 1972 as Queens Center for Art and Culture in the New York City Building for the 1938 World Fair: redesigned by Rafael Viñoly in 1994): New York City Building at Flushing Meadows Corona Park in Queens, NY 11368

**Whitney Museum of American Art** (founded by Gertrude Vanderbilt Whitney (1907–1942) in 1914): current Marcel Breuer Building since 1966 on Madison Avenue at 75th Street; Nam June Paik (1982)

**Whitney Museum of American Art at Philip Morris** (later called Altria): opened in 1982 and closed in 2007/2008; located at 42nd Street near Grand Central Terminal; Ik-joong Kang (1996); Byron Kim (1999)

## SECTION 3: ASSOCIATIONS (1980s - 1990s)

As more and more immigrants arrived from Korea, many clubs and societies for art and culture sprang up in metropolitan areas where Korean population is dense. In New York area, there are half dozen associations of amateur and professional artists. They have two to four exhibitions each year.

***Hoyeon Hoe* 호연회** Promoting Korean traditional ink painting; located in Queens, NY

Korean-American Artist Associates

**(뉴욕한인현대미술협회)** Located in Queens, NY

Korean-American Contemporary Arts, Ltd.

**(한미현대미술가협회)** Composed of artists interested in Korean traditional ink painting, oil painting, calligraphy, photography, sculpture, installation, dance, and theatre

**Korean-American Traditional Artists Association (재미한국화가 협회)** Promoting and creating Korean traditional art; located in North Wales, Pennsylvania

***Nokmee* (녹미회)** Women artists graduated from Ehwa Womans University working and living in New York and East Coast

# APPENDIX 3: IMPORTANT EXHIBITIONS IN THE 1980s and 1990s

This list is far from complete. *The Faces and Facts* catalogue has a similar list of exhibitions. Nonetheless, this working list of exhibitions may still be useful in viewing the many exhibitions organized by or for Korean-American artists. Entries in red signify that posters or catalogues are in the collection of Sung-ho Choi and also in the Archive of Korean-American Artists at the AHL Foundation.

1981 Exhibition "Korean Drawing Now" (47 Korean and Korean American Artists), Brooklyn Museum, Brooklyn, June 27-September 7, 1981

1982 Opening of the Storefront for Art and Architecture by Kyong Park in the Lower East Side, New York

1982 Exhibition "Contemporary Korean Painting" at Sarah Lawrence College, Bronxville, NY November 16-December 12, 1982

1984 Letter to Minor Injury

1984 Name June Paik, "Good Morning, Mr. Orwell," a satellite project in NY, Paris, South Korea, and Germany, January 1, 1984

1985 Opening of Minor Injury by Mo Bahc, Brooklyn, NY 1985

1985 Roots to Reality: Asian America in Transition at Henry Street Settlement

1985 Nam June Paik at John Pai's New Year's Party, Brooklyn

1986 Exhibition "Korea / New York 86: 12 Artists from the Metropolitan Area" (12 Korean artists), Thorpe Intermedia Gallery, Sparkill, NY (catalogue) 12 artists from Korea

1986 New York's Current Korean Art, Gallery Korea (New York)

1986 Nam June Paik, "Bye Bye Kipling," a satellite project in New York, Seoul, and Tokyo, October 4, 1986

1988 Exhibition "Immigration" (more than 50 Korean and Korean American artists) at Alpine Gallery, New York, October 14-November 5, 1988 (Taewon Kim) 1988 Exhibition "Min Joong Art: A New Cultural Movement from Korea" at Artists Space, New York, September 29-November 5, 1988 (poster)

1988 Exhibition "Korea Art Today" at the Asian American Art Centre

1990 Mosaic of the City: Artists against Racial Prejudice (poster)

1990 Exhibition "The Decade Show: Frameworks of Identity in the 1980s" at the Hispanic Museum, the New Museum, and the Studio Museum, New York, May-August 19, 1990

1990 SEORO Korean Cultural Network founded, New York, August 5, 1990

1992 Seoro Korean Cultural Network (letter)

1992 Exhibition "A World Together, Korean Art, from Seoul, Paris, and New York" at the New York City Community Gallery (organized by the Korean Cultural Service NY and the Museum of the City of New York), April 4-June 28, 1992 1992 East and West, Invited Artists Exhibition, Haenah-Kent Gall (New York) (Chong Gon Byun)

1993 Public art by Sung-ho Choi

1994 Exhibition "Across the Pacific: Contemporary Korean and Korean American Art" at Queens Museum of Art, Queens, October 15, 1993-January 9, 1994

1994 Exhibition of "Asia / America: Identities in Contemporary Asian American Art" at the Asia Society Galleries, New York, February 16-June 26, 1994 (catalogue)

1996 Exhibition "Asian Traditions/Modern Expressions: Asian American Artists and Abstraction, 1945-1970" at Jane Voorhees Zimmerli Art Museum, Rutgers University, New Brunswick, NJ, March 23-July 31, 1997

1996 Exhibition "In the Eye of the Tiger" at Exit Art, New York, May 28-July 5, 1997 (10 Korean artists)

1996 Exhibition "Traditions/Tensions: Contemporary Art in Asia," Asia Society Galleries, Grey Art Gallery of New York University, and Queens Museum of Art, October 3, 1996-January 5, 1997 [Cho Duk Hyun; Choi Jeong-Hwa; Kim Ho-Suk; Soo-Ja Kim; Yun Suknam; Jae-Ryung Roe (art critic)]

1999 Exhibition "Global Conceptualism: Points of Origin 1950-1980" at Queens Museum of Art, New York, April 28-April 29, 1999

# APPENDIX 4: TIMELINE OF IMPORTANT EVENTS FOR KOREAN - AMERICAN ARTISTS: 1945–1999

| YEAR | ARTISTS ARRIVING IN THE US / New York | EXHIBITION | HISTORICAL EVENTS |
|---|---|---|---|
| 1945 | | | End of World War II |
| 1945 –1949 | | | Korea Divided into North and South |
| 1950 | | Exhibition "Korea: The Impact of War in Photographs" at the Museum of Modern Art | |
| 1952 | | | |
| 1953 | | | Armistice of Korean War |
| 1955 | Po Kim (b. 1917) came to the US on a fellowship at University of Illinois | | Montgomery Bus Boycott by Rosa Parks |
| 1956 | | | Founding Asia Society |
| 1957 | Po Kim came to New York | | Founding Asia Society |
| 1958 | John Pai (b. 1937) entered Pratt institute. | "Contemporary Korean Paintings" World House Galleries in New York organized by Ellen D. Psaty (Whanki Kim, Hun Kim, Byung-ki Kim and 32 others) | The Solomon R. Guggenheim Museum, designed by Frank Lloyd Wright (1867–1959), opens in New York. |
| 1959 | | | |
| 1960 | | | (Korea) 4.19 Revolution |
| 1961 | | | (Korea) 5.16 Military Coup by General Chung-hee Park |
| 1962 | Theresa Hak Kyung Cha (1951–1982) and her family arrived in the U.S. | Dongkuk Ahn (Don Ahn) goes to Korea Art Exhibition at Seattle World's Fair. | Andy Warhol (1928–1987) paints Campbell's Soup Cans, a key work of the Pop Art movement. |
| 1963 | Whan Ki Kim (1913–1974)<br>Yong Jin Han (b. 1934) | 7th Bienal de Saõ Paulo (Whanki Kim as commissioner; Yong Jin Han and others) | March on Washington for Jobs and Freedom (August)<br>Assassination of John F. Kennedy (November) |

| | | | |
|---|---|---|---|
| 1964 | Nam June Paik (1932–2006)<br>Mi-aie Moon (1937–2004)<br>Byoung-ok Min (b. 1941) | | Civil Rights Act of 1964 |
| 1965 | | 8th Bienal de Saõ Paulo (Byungki Kim as commissioner;Tchang-yeul Kim and others)<br>Nam June Paik, Galeria Bonino, New York: first solo exhibition of "Electronic Art" in the US | |
| 1966 | | | Whitney Museum of Art moving to Marcel Breuer Building on Madison Avenue |
| 1967 | | Nong (Robert Han), Georgia Museum of Art, University of Georgia, Athens | *Artforum* (est. 1962) moving to New York |
| 1968 | Dorothy Deon (Ok-ji Kim; b. 1946) | | Assassination of Martin Luther King, Jr. |
| 1969 | | | Apollo 11 is launched from Cape Kennedy in Florida<br><br>(Korea) National Museum of Contemporary Art, Korea opened in Gyeongbokgung Palace |
| 1970 | Woong Kim (b. 1944) | | Robert Smithson's (1938–1973) earth-art *Spiral Jetty* at Great Salt Lake in Utah |
| 1971 | | Whanki Kim, Poindexter Gallery, New York<br><br>Choong Sup Lim, O.I.A. Group Show, P.S. 1, Long Island City, NY | Linda Nochlin, "Why Have There Been No Great Women Artists?" (*ART News*, (January 1971) |
| 1972 | Woon Suk Kim (b. 1953)<br>Kyu Nam Han (b. 1945) | Kwang Young Chun, Holly Solomon Gallery (98 Greene Street Loft at the time) New York | Founding Queens Museum of Art (Queens Center for Art and Culture)<br>Irving Sandler founding Artists Space as alternative art space |
| 1973 | Choong Sup Lim (b. 1941) | Kyu Back Hwang's print is acquired by the Museum of Modern Art | U.S. troops withdraw from Vietnam |

| 1974 | Tchah Sup Kim<br>(b. 1940)<br>Chung Yoon Kim<br>(b. 1949) | | Judy *Chicago, Dinner* Party<br>(1974–1979) |
|---|---|---|---|
| 1975 | Il Dan Choi (b. 1937) | Byoung-ok Min, Aldrich Museum Annual 1975, Aldrich Museum of Contemporary Art, Ridgefield, Connecticut | Henry Street Settlement Arts for Living Center |
| 1976 | Myong Hi Kim<br>(b. 1949) | Tchah Sup Kim, *Acquisitions* '73–'76 at the Museum of the Modern Art, New York<br>Nam June Paik, Retrospective at Kolnischer Kunstverein, Cologne (Germany) | Alex Haley (1921–1992) publishes *Roots*, popular novel documenting the historical experience of African Americans<br>*October* (journal) founded by Rosalind Krauss and Annette Michelson |
| 1977 | Jung Hyang Kim<br>(b. 1955)<br>Il Lee (b. 1952) | | Marcia Tucker founding New Museum of Contemporary Art |
| 1978 | | | |
| 1979 | Mikyung Kim (b. 1956) | Korean Cultural Service in New York is founded. | (Korea) Assassination of President Chung-hee Park |
| 1980 | Theresa Hak Kyung Cha (1951–1982) came to New York | Six Artists, Hankook Gallery, New York, NY | (Korea) Gwangju Democratic Movement<br>Neo-Expressionist movement in the 1980s: Julian Schnabel (b. 1951), David Salle (b.1952), Eric Fischl (b.1948), and others |
| 1981 | Joseph Pang (b. 1965)<br>Chong Gon Byun<br>(b. 1948)<br>Soo Im Lee (b. 1954)<br>Sang Nam Lee<br>(b. 1953)<br>Sung Ho Choi<br>(b. 1954) | "Korean Drawing Now"<br>(47 Korean and Korean American Artists), Brooklyn Museum, Brooklyn, June 27–September 7<br>Smithsonian Institute Traveling Exhibition Service, Washington, DC<br>Choong Sup Lim goes to "Annual Juried Exhibition '80" at Queens Museum, New York<br>Tchah-sup Kim goes to "30 Years of American Printmaking" at Brooklyn Museum, New York | Richard Serra installs his sculpture *Tilted Arc* in Federal Plaza, New York |

| 1982 | Mo Bahc (1957–2004; 1982–1994 in NYC) | "Name June Paik" Whitney Museum of Art, new York, April 30–June 27<br>"Traditional Korean Pottery; Contemporary Korean Painting" at Sarah Lawrence College Art Gallery, Bronxville, NY( Il Lee, Boon-ja Choi, Kyu-nam Han, Tchah-sup Kim, and others)<br>Mikyung Kim, New Dimensions in Clay, Brooklyn Museum, Brooklyn, NY | Whitney Museum of American Art opening a performance space at Philip Morris |
|---|---|---|---|
| 1983 | | Two-persons exhibition: Mikyung Kim and Woong Kim, P.S. 122 (Painting Space 122), New York, NY | |
| 1984 | Ik-Joong Kang (b. 1960)<br>Seung Lee (b. 1960) | Name June Paik, "Good Morning, Mr. Orwell," a satellite project in NY, Paris, South Korea, and Germany on January 1, 1984<br>Mikyung Kim, "For Distant Viewing" at Battery Park City Landfill (with architect Michel Kagan; dancer Lisa Kraus; composer John Hagen) | Asian American Arts Centre (est. 1974) starting art exhibition program |
| 1985 | | Opening of Minor Injury by Mo Bahc, Brooklyn, NY 1985<br>"Roots to Reality: Asian America in Transition" at Henry Street Settlement | Noguchi Museum opens in Long Island City |
| 1986 | Yeong Gill Kim (b. 1957) | Exhibition "Korea/New York 86: 12 Artists from the Metropolitan Area" (12 Korean artists), Thorpe Inter media Gallery, Sparkill, NY<br>Gallery Korea opens at the Korean Cultural Service | (Korea) National Museum of Contemporary Art, Korea moved to Gwacheon |

| 1987 | | | (Korea) June Democratic Uprising |
|---|---|---|---|
| 1988 | Sook Jin Jo (b. 1960) | "Min Joong Art: A New Cultural Movement from Korea" at Artists Space, New York "Korea Art Today" at the Asian American Art Centre<br><br>"Immigration" at Alpine Gallery, New York (more than 50 Korean and Korean-American artists) | (Korea) Seoul hosts the 24th Summer Olympic Games.<br><br>Alliance for Asian American Arts and Culture (est. 1970s) renamed as Asian American Artist Alliance |
| 1989 | Theresa Chong (b. 1965) | | Removal of Richard Serra' sculpture, *Tilted Arc*, after a notorious lawsuit |
| 1990 | | SEORO Korean Cultural Network founded in New York on August 5, 1990 by Mo Bahc, Sung Ho Choi, and Hae Jung Park.<br><br>"Mosaic of the City: Artists against Racial Prejudice" at the Center for Art and Culture of Bedford Stuyvesant, (Yongsoon Min, Mo Bahc, Sung Ho Choi, Tae Ho Lee, David Chung, Yeong Gill Kim, and Ho Yoon Choi)<br><br>"The Decade Show: Frameworks of Identity in the 1980s" at the Hispanic Museum, the New Museum, and the Studio Museum, New York (Yongsoon Min and David Chung) | Boycott of a Korean-owned Family Red Apple Market in Flatbush, Brooklyn<br>Gulf War (1990–1991) |
| 1991 | | "24 Korean Artists in New York" at Haenah-Kent Gallery, New York | |

| | | | |
|---|---|---|---|
| 1992 | | "A World Together, Korean Art, from Seoul, Paris, and New York" at the New York City Community Gallery (organized by the Korean Cultural Service NY and the Museum of the City of New York)<br>"David Chung: Turtle Boat Head" at Whitney Museum of American Art, New York<br>"3x3" of Ik-Joong Kang" at Queens Museum of Art, New York | Los Angeles Riots (Rodney King Riots) |
| 1993 | Sook Jin Jo (b. 1960) | Byron Kim contributed *Synecdoche* (1991–92) to Whitney Biennial<br><br>"Across the Pacific: Contemporary Korean and Korean American Art" at Queens Museum of Art, New York | |
| 1994 | | "Asia/America: Identities in Contemporary Asian American Art" at the Asia Society Galleries, New York | Removal of Richard Serra' sculpture, *Tilted Arc*, after a notorious lawsuit |
| 1995 | | "Passion and Compassion," Asian American Arts Center, New York | Korean Pavilion established at the Venice Biennale.<br>"The Tiger's Tail" exhibition was held to commemorate the foundation of the Korean Pavilion.<br>(Korea)The first Gwangju Biennale<br>Chang-rae Lee (b. 1965), *Native Speaker* |
| 1996 | | "In the Eye of the Tiger" at Exit Art, New York (Choong Sup Lim, Sook Jin Jo, 8 Others)<br><br>"Traditions/Tensions: Contemporary Art in Asia" at Asia Society Galleries, Grey Art Gallery of New York University, and Queens Museum of Art (Jeong-hwa Choi, Kim Sooja, Duck Hyun Cho, Suknam Yun)<br><br>"Ik-Joong Kang: 8490 Days of Memory" at Whitney Museum of American Art, New York | |

| 1997 | | "Asian Traditions/Modern Expressions: Asian American Artists and Abstraction, 1945–1970" at Jane Voorhees Zimmerli Art Museum, Rutgers University, New Brunswick, NJ (Dong Kuk Ahn, Nong Han, Po Kim, Whanki Kim, and others) | |
|---|---|---|---|
| 1998 | | | Permanent "Arts of Korea" Gallery at the Metropolitan Museum of Art |
| 1999 | | "Global Conceptualism: Points of Origin 1950–1980" at Queens Museum of Art, New York<br><br>"Confluence of Cultures" at Gallery Korea, New York | "Sensation" at Brooklyn Museum (protest on the Holy Virgin Mary by Chris Ofili) |

# APPENDIX 5: EXHIBITION VIEWS OF *COLORING TIME* AT KOREAN CULTURAL SERVICE

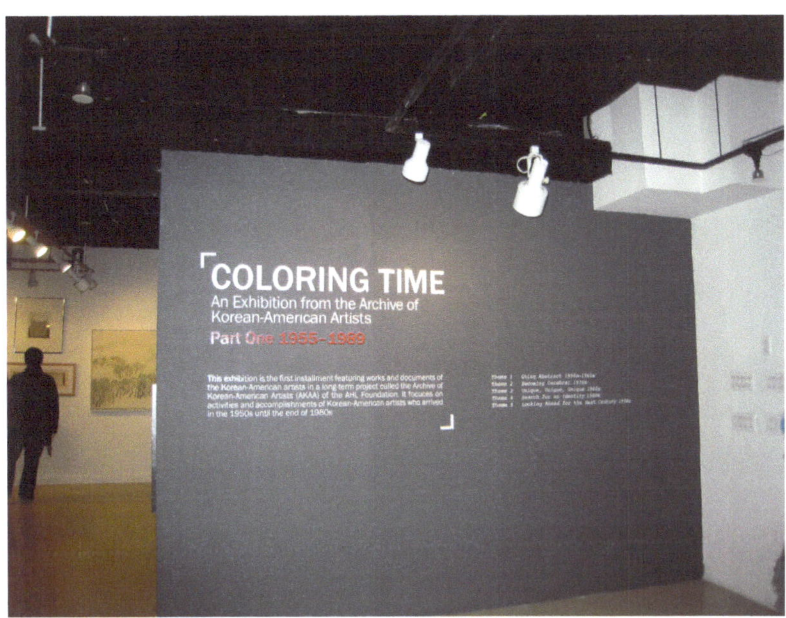


**Plate A-1** Photograph of the Exhibition Title, *Coloring Time*

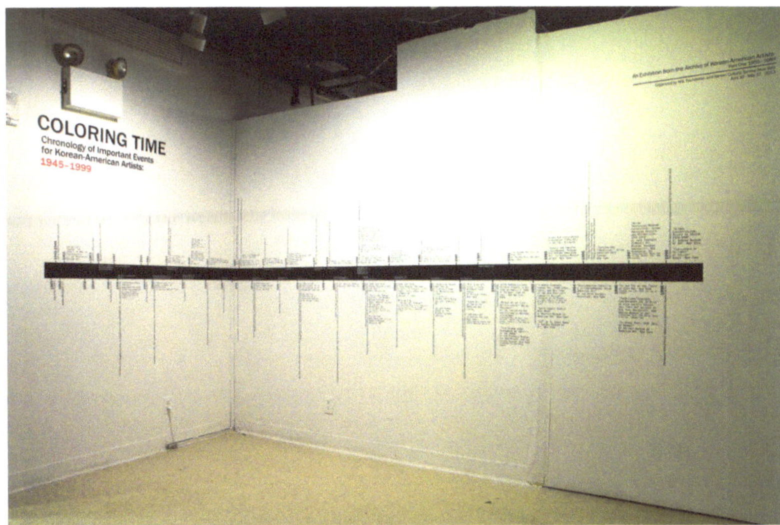


**Plate A-2** Photograph of the Timetable for *Coloring Time*

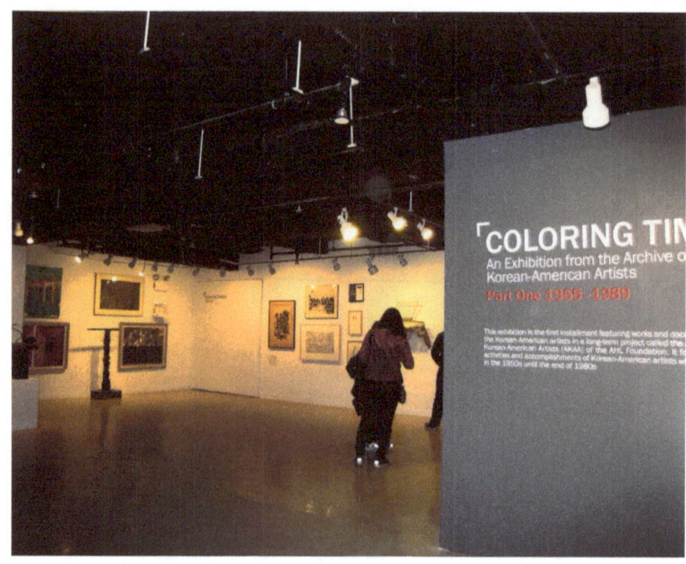


**Plate B-1** Photograph of the Exhibition: Whole View to the Right from the Entrance

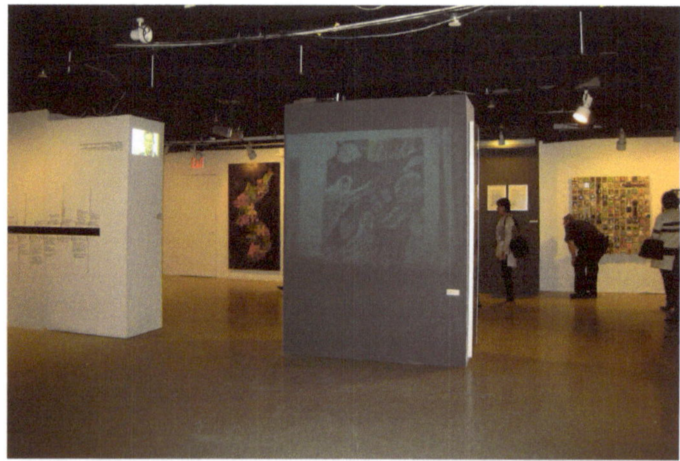

**Plate B-2** Photograph of the Exhibition: Whole View to the Left from the Entrance

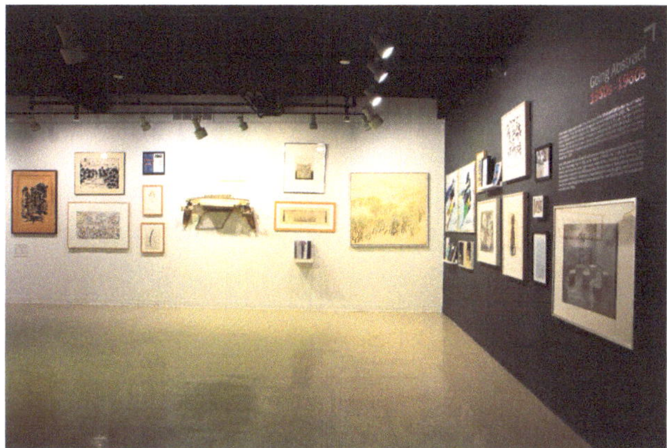

**Plate C-1** Photograph of Theme 1 and Theme 2 of *Coloring Time*

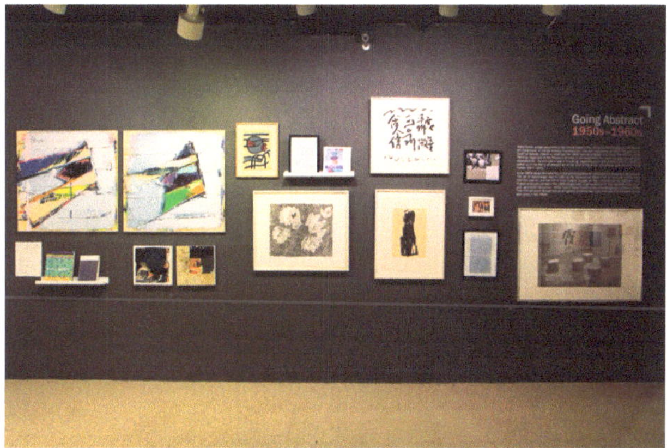

**Plate C-2** Photograph of "Theme 1: Going Abstract 1950s-1960s" of *Coloring Time*

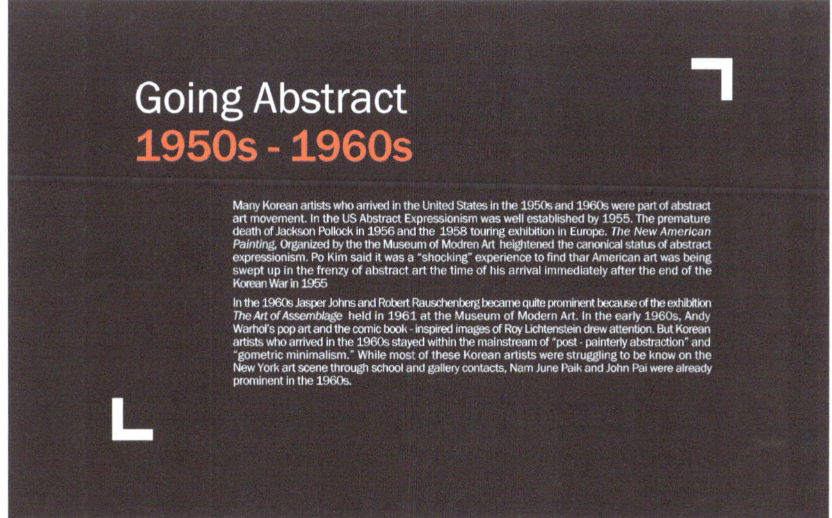


**Plate C-3** Wall Text of "Theme 1: Going Abstract 1950-1960s" of *Coloring Time*

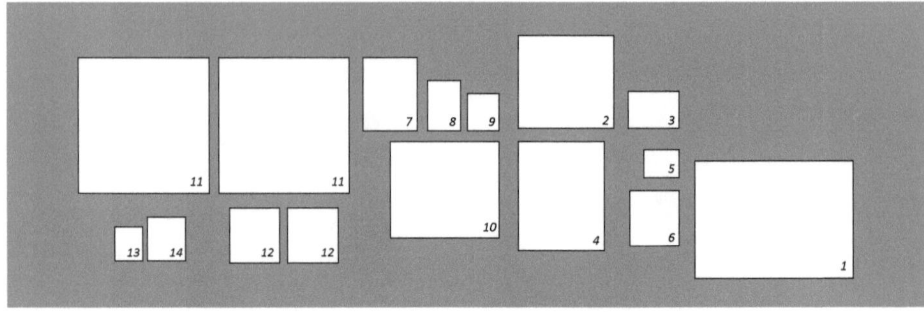


1 Poster of an exhibition Nam June Pailk and Han Yong Jin at Sigma Gallery, 1995
Collection: AHL Foundation Archive of Korean-American Artists

2 Nam June Paik
*Untitled,* 1989
Ink on paper, 17. 8 x 19.5 inches
Collection: Mrs. Sook Nyu Lee Kim

3 Photo of Nam June Paik with Young Korean-American Artists (taken by Sung Ho Choi)
Collection: AHL Foundation Archive of Korean-American Artists

4 Han Yong Jin
*Untitled,* 1997
Lithograph on paper, 40 x 28 inches
Collection: Artist

5 Photo of Yong Jin Han with Young Korean-American Artists (Sung Ho Choi and Daru-Jung Yang Kim)
Collection: AHL Foundation Archive of Korean-American Artists

6 Incomplete Letter of Yong Jin Han, 11 November 1997
Describing his unfailing passion for art

7 Whanki Kim
*Mountain and Moon,* 1964.
Gouache on paper, 11.75 x 8.5 inches
Collection: Mrs. Sook Nyu Lee Kim

8 Letter of Mrs. Hyang-an Kim (Whanki Kim's wife) to Mrs. Sook Nyu Lee Kim, owner of Hankook Gallery, 28 April 1980
Collection: AHL Foundation Archive of Korean-American Artists

9 Catalogue of "Whanki" Selected Works 1965-1970 at Poindexter Gallery, 1977
Collection: AHL Foundation Archive of Korean-American Artists

10 John Pai
*Untitled,* 1985
Print, 30 x 24 inches
Collection Ms. Eun Young Kang

11 Byoung Ok Min
*Tide,* 1986
Wood, canvas strips, acrylic on canvas, 31 x 32 inches
Collection: Artist

12 Po Kim
*Small Collage 12,* 1979-1980
Mixed media, 12 x 12 inches
Collection: Artist

13 Matthew Kim
*Memoir of Matthew Kim: Korean Modern and Contemporary Artists I loved,* Seoul: Ji-wa-Sarang, 2012
Collection: AHL Foundation Archive of Korean-American Artists

14 Catalogue of *Remembering Mi-aie Moon* at Whanki Museum in Seoul, 2008
Collection: AHL Foundation Archive of Korean-American Artists

**Plate C-4** Diagram of Art Works with Captions of "Theme 1: Going Abstract 1950-1960s" of *Coloring Time*

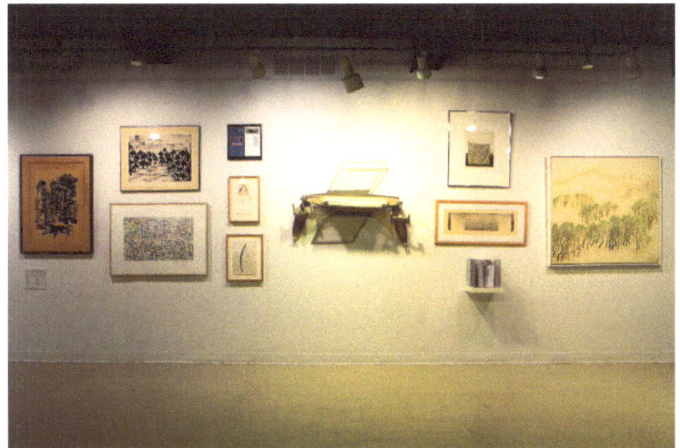

**Plate D-1** Photograph 1 of "Theme 2: Becoming Cerebral 1970s" of *Coloring Time*

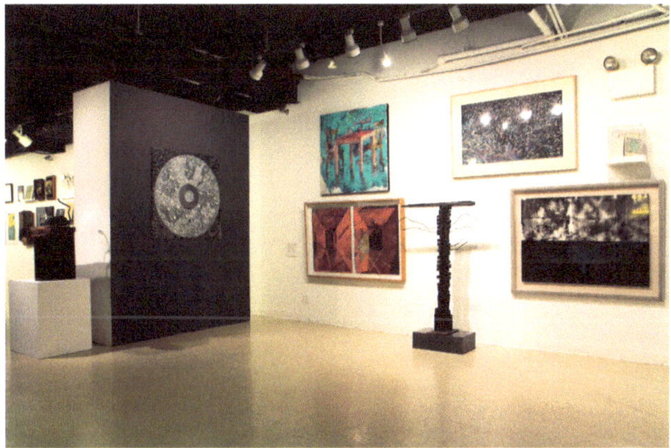

**Plate D-2** Photograph 2 of "Theme 2: Becoming Cerebral 1970s" of *Coloring Time*

## Becoming Cerebral
## 1970s

The 1970s was a tubulent time resulting in the coexistence of established style of abstract and minimalist art along with the emergence of several new style, including, conceptual art, earth art, and body art (which was often informed by feminist art practice). Art works or projects became public oriented or socially engaged in the political climate represented by the civil rights moment women's right, and the anti - Vietnam War movements. This spirit of anti - establishment was favorable to Korean or Korean - American artists. Those who arrived in the 1960s were more visible in gallery space, and young artists also found an audience. Also Korean artists who came to the US in the 1970s reflected more diverse styles of installations, mixed - media art, and prints. These intellectual artists from this period experimented with new possibilities in forms and aesthetics while looking for their authentic voice and re - discovering cultural heritage as Koreans.

*'My twenties were all about America. [...] The American dream promised success and weath, but the reality was that some innocent youth in every other house were dying on the battlefield.'*

*'Abstract Expressionism was best to express the chaos and struggles of the world I lives in, but my 'artistic fastidiousness' undermined my devotion to this art form. [...] The image of cursed artists who endlessly painted second - rate imitations in a gloomy studio started to haunt me and I felt devastated. Why can't I just compromise with reality? How can I find the best way to express my art? How can I, as Korean artist, create my own original style?'* __Kwang Young Chun (b.1944, in the US in the 1970s)

**Plate D-3** Wall Text of "Theme 2: Becoming Cerebral 1970s" of *Coloring Time*

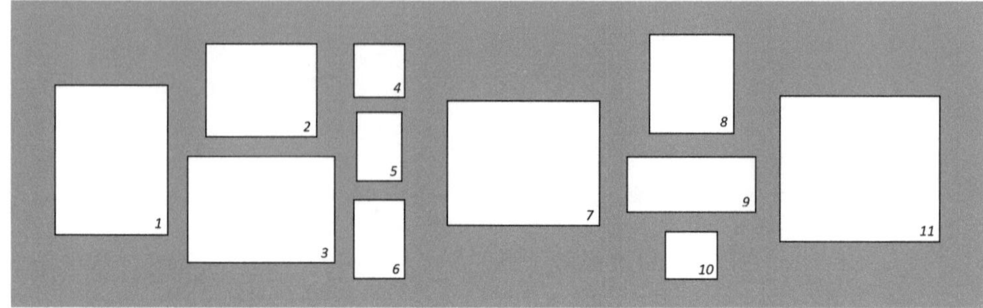


1 Elaine Il Dan Choe
*Trilport* (outside Paris), 1973
Ink and color on paper, 40 x 28 inches
**Collection: Artist**

2 Wonsook Kim
*To Our House*, 1976
Lithograph on paper, 17.5 x 23.8 inches
**Collection: Artist**

3 Kyu Nam Han
*Untitled,* 1980s
Oil on canvas, 37 x 27 inches
**Collection: Ms. Eun Young Kang**

4 Poster of ***Queens Artists***
*: Highlights of the 20th Century* at Queens Museum of Art, 1997
[Choong Sup Lim]

5 Choong Sup Lim
*Drawing,* 1995
Pencil on paper, 6 x 11 3/8 inches
**Collection: Artist**

6 Choong Sup Lim
*Drawing,* 1995
Pencil on paper, 8 3/8 x 12 inches
**Collection: Artist**

7 Choong Sup Lim
*Ta - Rae (Spindle),* 1995
Threads, acrylic, wood, rice paper, U. V. L. S gel, 32 x 45 x 15 inches
**Collection: Artist**

8 Kyu Back Hwang
*Handkerchief on the Grass,* 1979
Print, 24 x 16 inches
**Collection: Mrs. Sook Nyu Lee Kim**

9 Tchah Sup Kim
*Untitled,* 1975
Etching print on paper, 9 x 29 inches
**Collection: Artist**

10 Tchah Sup Kim
Four Drawing Books, 2005-2006; 2006; 2006-2007; 2007-2008
Pencil and pen on paper, each 5 7/8 x 8 5/8 inches
**Collection: Artist**

11 Dong Kuk Ahn (Don Ahn)
*Untitled,* ca. 1968-1972
Acrylic on canvas, 45.5 x 41.5 inches
Courtesy of Walter Wickiser Gallery

**Plate D-4**
Diagram of Art Works with Captions of "Theme 2: Becoming Cerebral 1970s" of *Coloring Time* (continued on the next page)

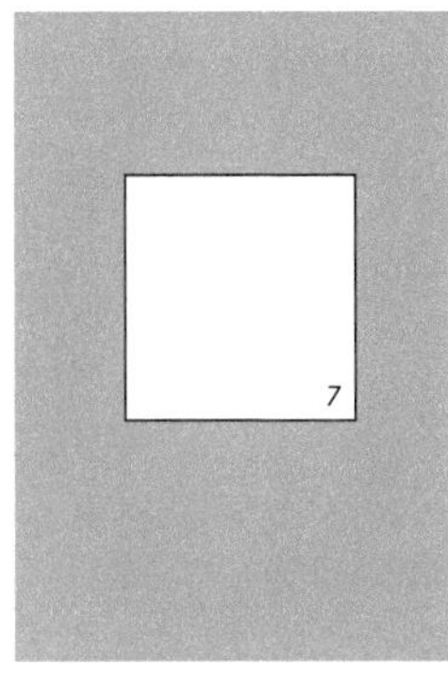


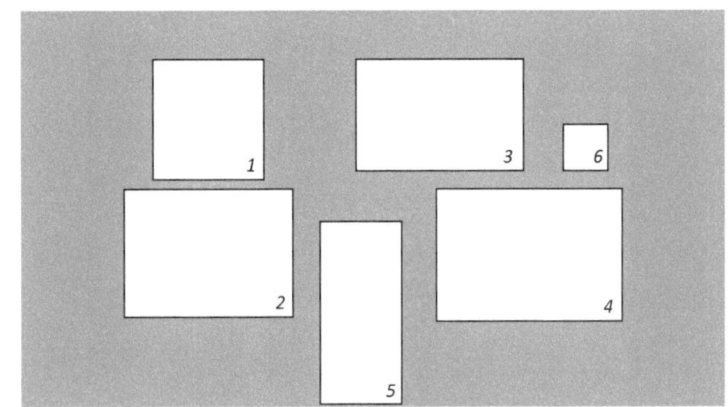


1 Yuran Lee
*Whispering Wood #1,* 1998
Acrylic on canvas, 36 x 36 inches
Collection: Artist

2 Woong Kim
*Red interior,* 1981
Oil on canvas, 29 x 44 inches
Collection: Artist

3 Boon Ja Choi
[Title unknown], 1982
Water color on rice paper, 47 x 32 inches
Collection: Ms. Eun Young Kang

4 Youn Hee Paik
*Ship-West,* 1997
Acrylic on paper, 30 x 42 inches
Collection: Artist

5 Chung Yoon Kim
*Untitled,* 1985
Wood and metal, 32 x 10 x 46 inches
Collection: Artist

6 Youn Hee Paik
Two Drawing Books, 1993 and 1997-1998
Pencil and pen on paper, 6 x 8 inches
Collection: Artist

7 Dorothy Deon (Ok Ji Kim)
*Oneness,* 2000
Mixed media on plastic, 36 x 36 inches
Collection: Artist

Chung Yoon Kim
*Untitled,* 1980
Stone, wood, and metal, 30 x 13 x 30 inches
Collection: Artist

(continued from the previous page)

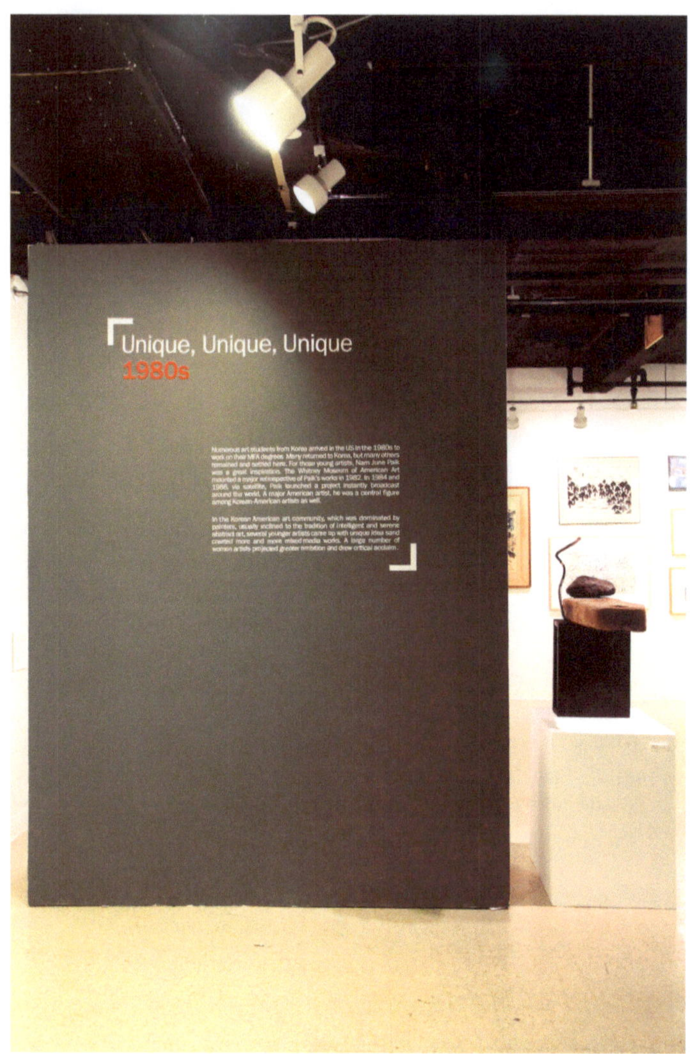


**Plate E-1** Photograph 1 of "Theme 3: Unique, Unique, Unique 1980s" of *Coloring Time*

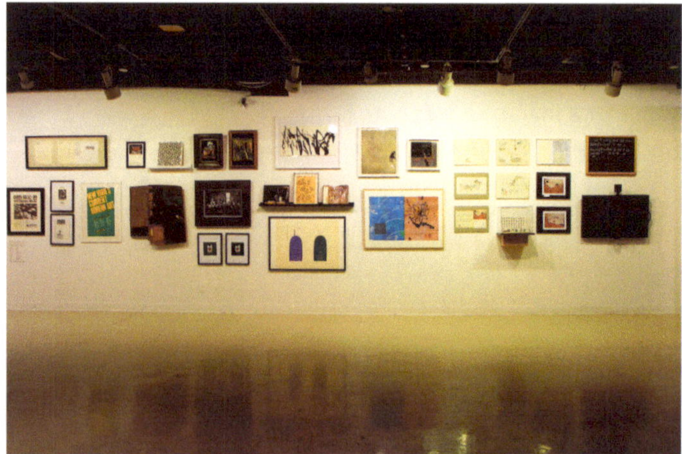

**Plate E-2** Photograph 2 of "Theme 3: Unique, Unique, Unique 1980s" of *Coloring Time*

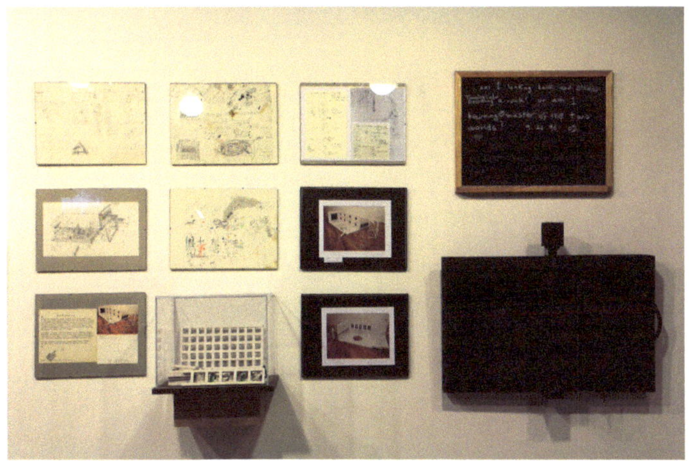

**Plate E-3** Photograph 3 of "Theme 3: Unique, Unique, Unique 1980s" of *Coloring Time*

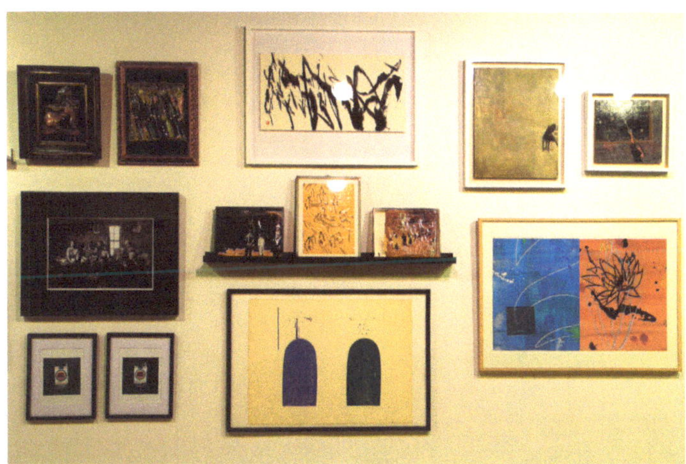

**Plate E-4** Photograph 4 of "Theme 3: Unique, Unique, Unique 1980s" of *Coloring Time*

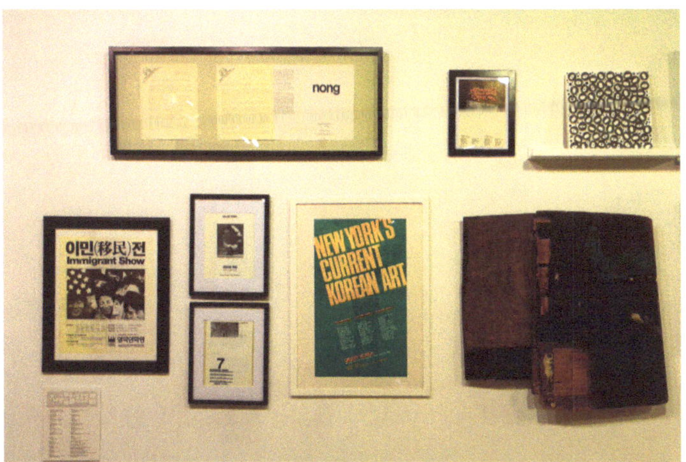


**Plate E-5** Photograph 5 of "Theme 3: Unique, Unique, Unique 1980s" of *Coloring Time*

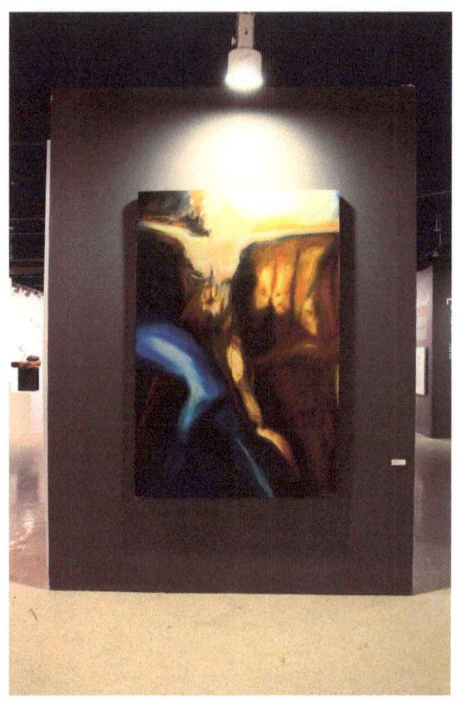

**Plate E-6**
Photograph 6 of "Theme 3: Unique, Unique, Unique 1980s" of *Coloring Time*

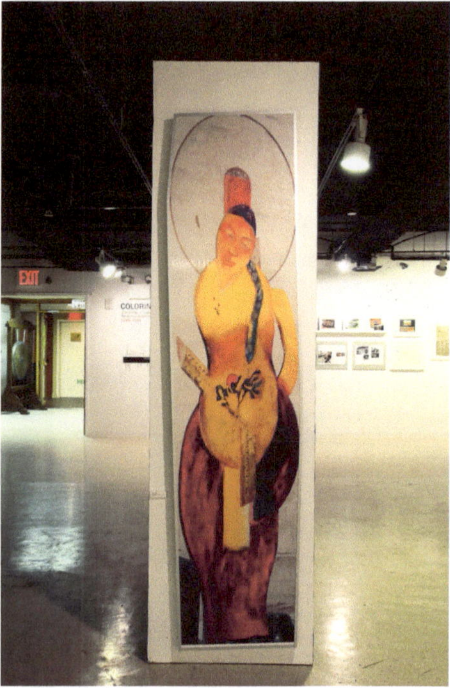

EXIT

**Plate E-7**
Photograph 7 of "Theme 3: Unique, Unique, Unique 1980s" of *Coloring Time*

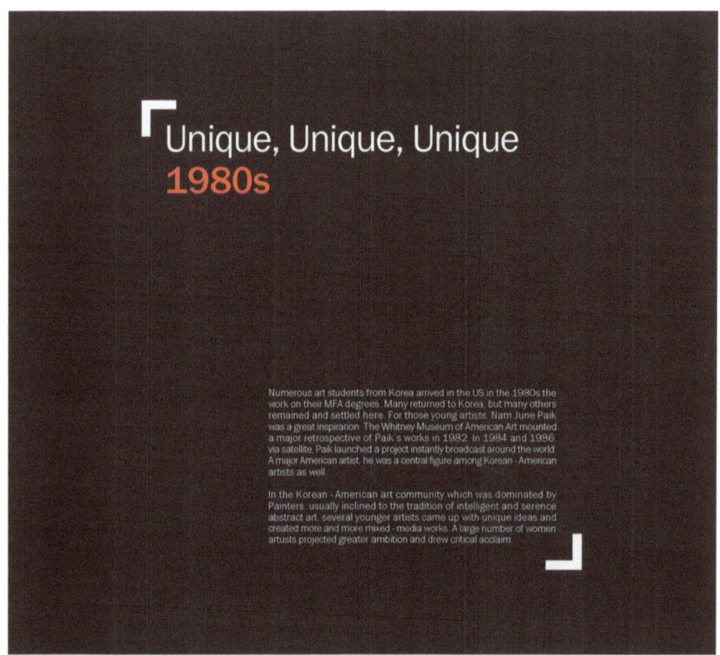

Unique, Unique, Unique
1980s
Numerous art students from Korea arrived in the US in the 1980s the work on their MFA degrees. Many returned to Korea, but many others remained and settled here. For those young artists, Nam June Paik was a great inspiranon. The Whitney Museum of American Art mounted a major retrospective of Paik's works in 1982. In 1984 and 1986, via satellite, Paik launched a project instantly broadcast around the world. A major American artist, he was a central figure among Korean - American artists as well.
In the Korean - American art community which was dominated by Painters, usually inclined to the tradition of intelligent and serence abstract art, several younger artists came up with unique ideas and created more and more mixed - media works. A large number of women artusts projected greater ambition and drew critical acclaim.

**Plate E-8** Wall Text of "Theme 3: Unique, Unique, Unique 1980s" of *Coloring Time*

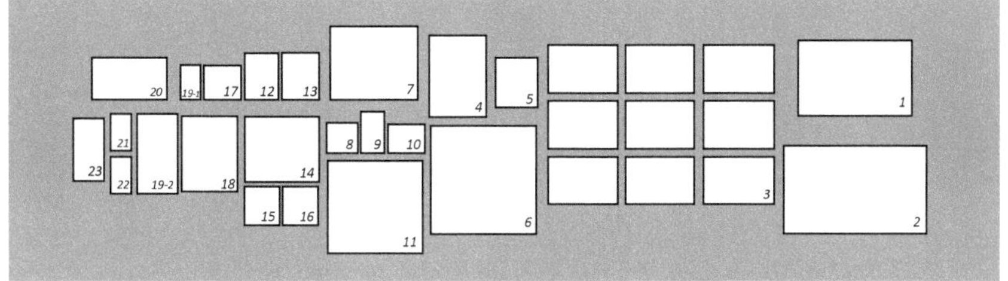


1 Myong Hi Kim
*Master of the Two Worlds,* 1996-1998
Oil-pastel on chalkboard, 18 x 24 inches
Collection: Artist

2 Chong Gon Byun
*Gold Ice Cream,* 1982
Mixed media, 24.5 x 32 x 6 inches
Collection: Artist

3 Mi Kyung Kim
Idea scathes, parts from ***Untitled 64,*** 1983
Acrylic on wood, 50 x 24 x 14 inches
Collection: Artist

4 Soo Im Lee
*Freeman at Corner,* 2002
Acrylic on woodblock, 20 x 16 inches
Collection: Artist

5 Soo Im Lee
*Pink Ball,* 1998
Acrylic on woodblock, 12 x 11 inches
Collection: Artist

6 Daru-Jung hyang Kim
*Lotus,* 1995
Mixed Medium on paper, 24 x 32 inches
Collection: Artist

7 Ju Sang Kim
*Strolling,* 2011
Ink on Korean rice paper, 14 x 24 inches
Collection: Artist

8 Yeong Gill Kim
*Father and Son,* 1991
Mixed Media, 10 x 12 inches
Collection: Artist

9 Yeong Gill Kim
*Old Box,* 1991
Mixed media, 10 x 12 inches
Collection: Artist

10 Yeong Gill Kim
***Untitled,*** 1993
Ink, wax on paper, 12 x 15 inches
Collection: Artist

11 Sung Hee Cho
An Illusion, 1981
Etching and mezzotint with colors, 37 x 30 inches
Collection: Mrs. Sook Nyu Lee Kim

12 Seung Lee
*Film Collaged Drawing in ZipLock Bag,* 1985-2005
Mixed media, 12 x 14 inches
Collection: Artist

13 Seung Lee
***Italy Painting,*** 1983 -2005
Mixed media, 12 x 14 inches
Collection: Artist

14 Jin Hong Kim
*People,* 1984
Kodak RC paper, 12x17 inches
Collection: Artist

15 Won Jun Park
*Lucky Strike with the Spider Man,* 1989
Digital photography, 11 x 8.5 inches
Collection: Artist

16 Won Jun Park
*Lucky Strike with Marilyn Monroe,* 1989
Digital photography, 11 x 8.5 inches
Collection: Family

17 Eung Ho Park
*Shocked,* 2012
Epoxy resin, oil and bottle caps on wood, 12 x 12 x 1 inches
Courtesy of Y Gallery New York

18 Sook Jin Jo
***Untitled,*** 2002
Oil on plywood, 2.5 x 29 x 3 inches
Collection: Artist

19 Poster of *New York's Current Korean Art* at Gallery Korea,
19-1 Collection: Korean Cultural Service New York
19-2 Collection: Il Dan Choi

20 Poster and Press Release of Nong Art Exhibition
at Korean Cultural Service, 1983
Collection: Korean Cultural Service New York

21 Poster of John Pai's *Root Images: Recent Welded Steel Sculpture*
at Gallery Korea, Korean Cultural Service, 1987
Collection: Korean Cultural Service New York

22 Poster of ***Seven Emerging Artists: Painting & Sculpture***
at Gallery Korea, Korean Cultural Service, 1987
[Young-Gill Kim, Myung Ah Lee; M Park; Seung Lee; Gwiwon Oh; Kyunghwa Park]
Collection: Korean Cultural Service New York

23 Poster of ***Immigration*** at Alpine Gallery, New York, 1988
More than 50 Korean and Korean American artists
Collection: Sung Ho Choi

| H. S. Sunny Soe<br>*The Mother,* 2003<br>Oil on panel with mixed media, 8.5 x 2 feet<br>Collection: Artist | Joseph Pang<br>*Epiphany in Passion,* 1987<br>Oil on canvas, 39 x 56 Inches<br>Collection: Artist |
|---|---|

**Plate E-9** Diagram of Art Works with Captions of "Theme 3: Unique, Unique, Unique 1980s" of *Coloring Time*

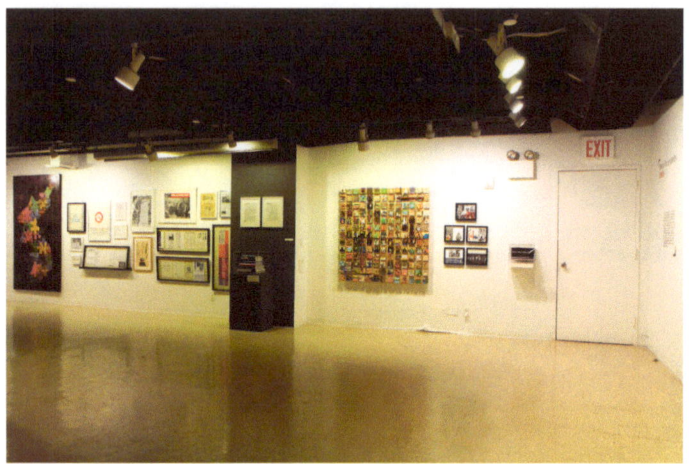


**Plate F-1** Photograph 1 of "Theme 4: Search for an Identity 1980s" of *Coloring Time*

# Search for an Identity
# 1980s

*"Then I grew older and began to read about adventures in which I didn't know that I was supposed to be on the side of those savages who were encountered by the good white man. [...] That was the way I was introduced to the danger of not having your own stories. There is that great proverb—that until the lions have their own historians, the history of the hunt will always glorify the hunter. [...] I had to be a writer. I had to be that historian. It's not one man's job. It's not one person's job. But it is something we have to do, so that the story of the hunt will also reflect the agony, the travail—the bravery, even, of the lions."—Chinua Achebe (1930-2013; Nigerian novelist), "The Art of Fiction" in The Paris Review (1994)*

In the 1980s a group of youn artists were searching for their identity and created their own art organizations. Sung Ho Choi founded SEORO Korean Cultural Network in 1990 with his friends and initiated a large - scale exhibition of Korean - American arists called *Across the Pacifix: Contemporary Korean and Korean - American Art at Queens Minor Injury, an alternative* art gallery for minority artists, in Brooklyn until 1989 while Chan Seung Jung was an idol among performing and media artists in association with Immersionism, a subculture growing out of warehouse art scenes in Williamsburg, Brooklyn.

**Plate F-2** Wall Text of "Theme 4: Search for an Identity 1980s" of *Coloring Time*

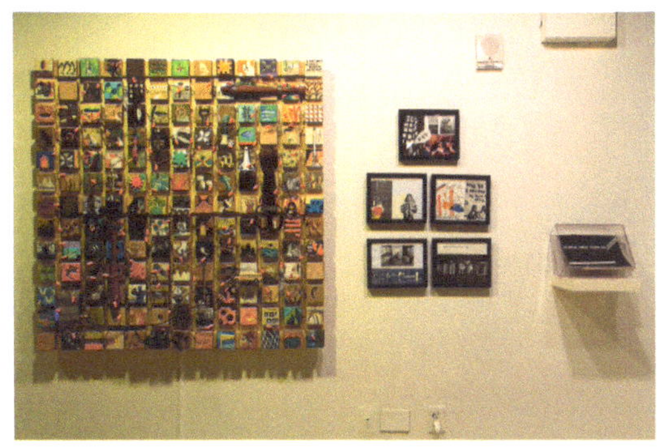

**Plate F-3**
Photograph 2 of "Theme 4: Search for an Identity 1980s" of *Coloring Time*

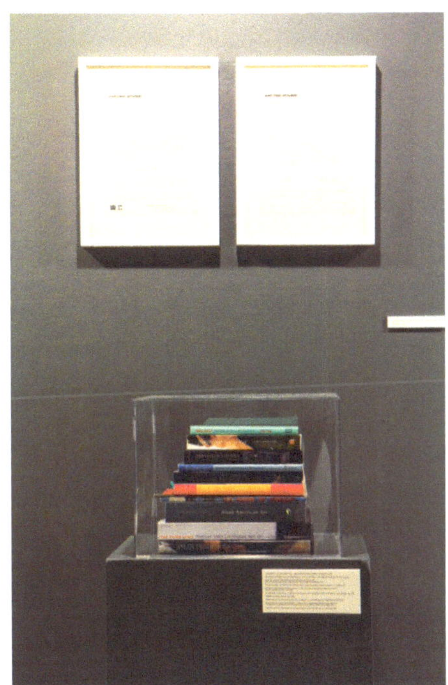

**Plate F-4**
Photograph 3 of "Theme 4: Search for an Identity 1980s" of *Coloring Time*

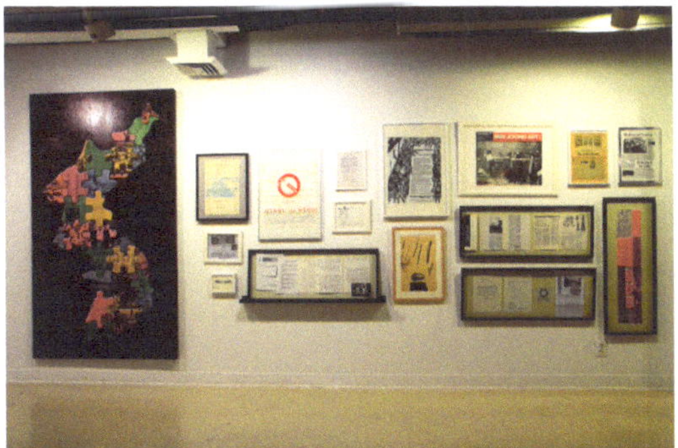

**Plate F-5**
Photograph 4 of "Theme 4: Search for an Identity 1980s" of *Coloring Time*

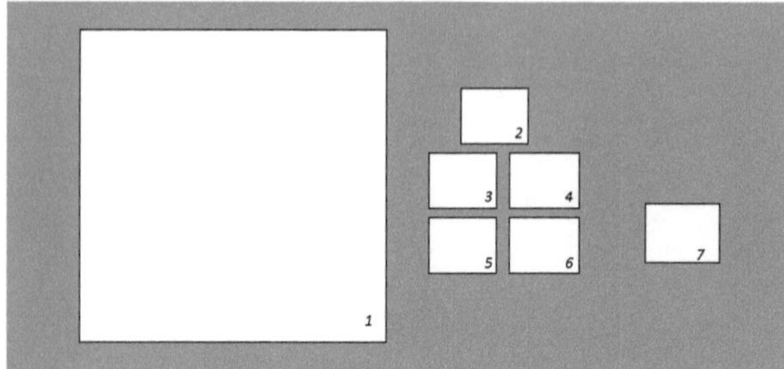


1 Ik-Joong Kang
Happy World, 1984-1990
Mixed media on wood, 51 x 51 inches
Collection: Artist

2 Photograph of Nam June Paik and Ik-Joong Kang
at Whitney Museum of American Art
at Champion in Stamford, CT in 1994
Collection: Artist

3 Ik-Joong Kang
Collage with Self Portrait, 1985
Collection: Artist

4 Ik-Joong Kang
"I Decided to Turn My Way" (1989) with a letter from E. A. "Tony" Mares and Kang's signature of 1986
Collection: Artist

5 Ik-Joong Kang
Photograph of *One Month Living Performance* at Two Two Row Gallery, New York, 1986
Collection: Artist

6 Ik-Joong Kang
Photograph of *Throw Everything Together and Add* for CAPP ST. Project, San Francisco, CA, 1994
Collection: Artist

7 Exhibition Catalogue of *Korean Drawing Now* at Brooklyn Museum, 1981/82
47 Korean and Korean American Artists
Collection: Sung Ho Choi
Exhibition Catalogue of *24 Korean Artists in New York* at Haenah-Kent Gallery, New York, 1991
Collection: Sung Ho Choi

Exhibition Announcement of *Roots for Reality: Asian America in Trasition* at Henry Street Settlement 1985
Colletion: Sung Ho Choi

Chang, Gordon H., et al. *Asian American Art: A history 1850-1970.* Stanford: Stanford University Press, 2008.

Chiu, Melissa, and Benjamin Genocchio. *Contemporary Art in Asia: A Critical Reader.* Cambridge, MA and London: The MIT Press, 2011.

Farver, Jane. *Across the Pacific: Contemporary Korean and Korean American Art.* New York: Queens Museum of Art in cooperation with SEORO Korean Cultural Network, 1993.

Hallmark, Kara Kelley. *Encyclopedia of Korean-American Artists: Artists of the American Mosaic.* Westport, CT: Greenwood, 2007.

Kim, Elaine H. Margo Machida, and Sharon Mizota. *Fresh Talk, Daring Gazes: Conversations on Asian American Art.* Berkeley: University of California Press, 2003.

Machida, Margo. *Unsettled Visions: Contemporary Asian American Artists and the Social Imaginary.* Durham, NC: Duke University Press, 2008.

*Minjoong Art* (catalogue) at Artists Space, 1988.

Munroe, Alexandra. *The Third Mind: American Artists Contemplate Asia, 1860-1989.* New York: Guggenheim Museum, 2009.

Wechsler, Michael, ed. *Asian Traditions/Modern Expressions: Asian American Artists and Abstraction, 1945–1970.* East Brunswick, NJ: Jane Voorhees Zimmerli Art Museum at the State University of New Jersey, Rutgers, 1997.

Yang, Alice. *Why Asia?: Contemporary Asian and Asian American Art.* New York: New York University Press, 1998.

**Plate F-6**

Diagram of Art Works with Captions of "Theme 4: Search for an Identity 1980s" of *Coloring Time* (continued on the next page)

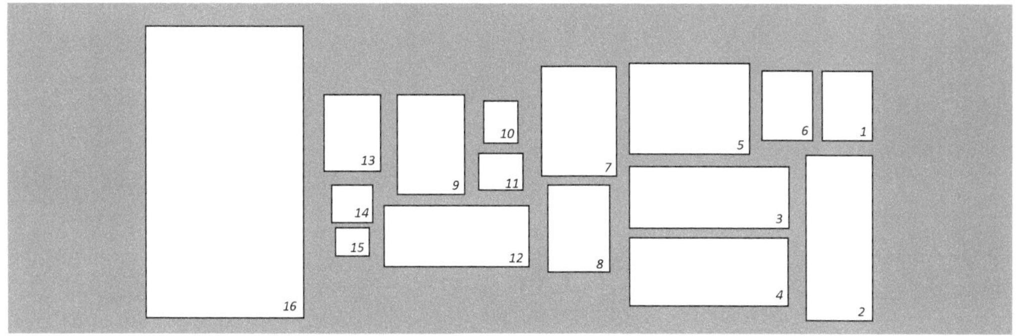


1 Review of the *Decade Show: Frameworks of Identity in the 1980s* at the Hispanic Museum, the New Museum, and the Studio Museum, New York in the Village Voice
Article of June 5, 1990 by Elizabeth Hess

2 Poster of the *Decade Show: Frameworks of Identity in the 1980s* at the Hispanic Museum, the New Museum, and the Studio Museum, New York
Collection: Sung Ho Choi

3 Two Reviews of the *Decade Show: Frameworks of Identity in the 1980s* at the Hispanic Museum, the New Museum, and the Studio Museum, New York in the New York Times
Article of May 25, 1990 by Roberta Smith
Article of May 27, 1990 by Michael Kimmelman

4 Documents of *Minor Injury* founded by Mo Bahc and Sam Binkley in 1985
1073 Manhattan Avenue in Greenpoint in 1985; 273 Grand Street in Williamsburg in 1990
Collection: Sung Ho Choi

5 Poster of Min Joong Art Exhibition, 1988
Collection: Sung Ho Choi

6 Review of *Min Joong Art: A New Cultural Movement from Korea* at Artists Space, New York in the Village Voice
Article of October 25, 1988 by Kim Levin

7 Poster of Afro-Asian Relations Council, 1995
Collection: Sung Ho Choi

8 Mo Bahc
Untitled Drawing, 1980s
Ink on paper, 18 x 12 inches
Collection: Daru-Jung Hyang Kim

9 Poster of *Mosaic of the City* Exhibition, 1990
Collection: Sung Ho Choi

10 Korean Translation of Afro-Asian Relations Council, 1995
Collection: Sung Ho Choi

11 Postcard of *Marginal Majority : Artists Against Racial Prejudice*
at Aaron Davis Hall of City College, 1991
Collection: Sung Ho Choi

12 List of Names and Documents of SEORO Korean Cultural Network, 1990
Collection: Sung Ho Choi

Foundation of SEORO Korean Cultural Network (handwriting by Mo Bahc), 1990
Collection: Sung Ho Choi

13 Poster of *Across the Pacific* at Queens Museum of Art, 1993/94
©AHL Foundation Archive of Korean-American Artists

14 Article on Mo Bahc and *Entrance of History/Historical Entrance,* mixed media, 1987
Article of Spring 1989 in the Village Voice Art Special by Holly Block

15 Postcard of *Meaning & Metaphor* at Space World Gallery, 1998
Four Korean-American Artists
Collection: Sung Ho Choi

16 Sung Ho Choi
*Their Korea,* 1994
Mixed media on wood, 84 x 48 inches
Collection: Artist

(continued from the previous page)

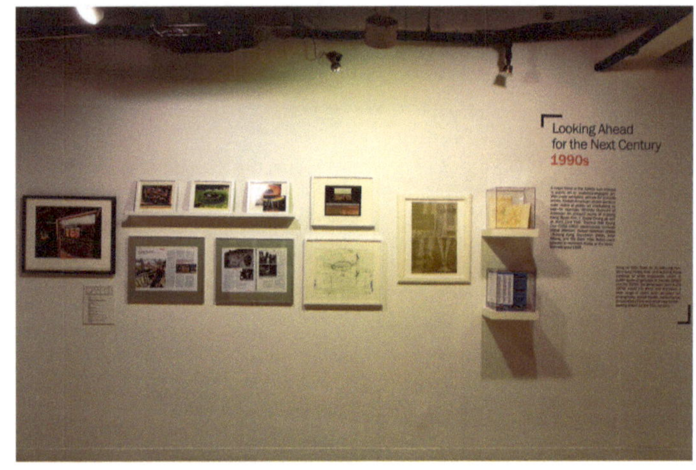


**Plate G-1**
Photograph 1 of "Theme 5: Looking Ahead for the Next Century 1990s" of *Coloring Time*

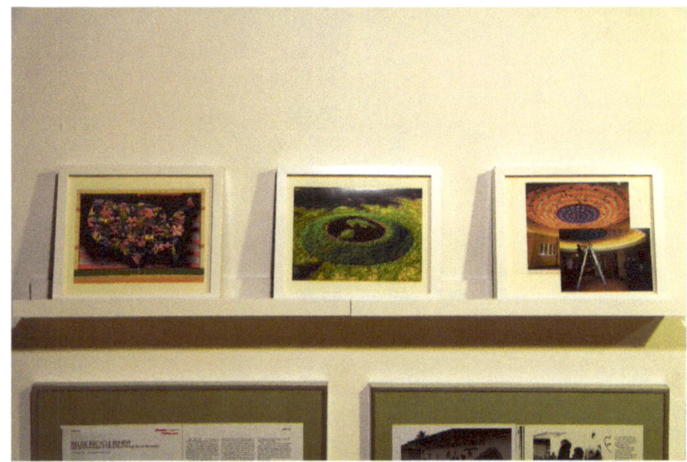

**Plate G-2**
Photograph 2 of "Theme 5: Looking Ahead for the Next Century 1990s" of *Coloring Time:* Sung Ho Choi's Public Art Projects

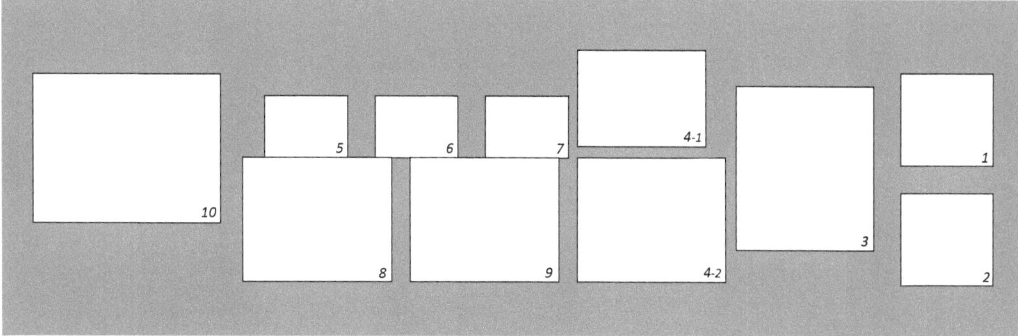


1 Mikyung Kim
Three Drawings of *Window #2* (proposal for a public art project), 1980s
Pencil on paper
Collection: Artist

2 Brochure of the *Percent for Art Program* by the Department of Cultural Affairs of New York City
For city agencies to acquire or commission works of art specifically for City-owned buildings since 1982/83
Korean artists included in "Artists with Completed Projects Commissioned by Percent for Art, 1985-2001
[Mo Bahc, Sung-Ho Choi, Ik-Joong Kang, and Yong Soon Min]

3 Poster of *Terminal New York*, 1983
Public Art Projects at the Former Brooklyn Army Terminal
Michael Keane and Kyung Park

4 Mikyung Kim
Drawing of For *Distant Viewing* at Battery Park City Landfill of New York, 1983
Collection: Artist

5 Sung Ho Choi
Photo of *My America,* 1996
Ceramic tile and silk screen, 92 x 144 inches
Public School I.S. 5 (Walter Crowley School) at 50-40 Jacobus Street, Queens, NY
Collection: Artist

6 Sung Ho Choi
Photo of *Morning Calm,* 1999
Mixed media, 23 x 23 x 2 feet
Warren G. Magnusson Park (former navy yard) at Sand Point Way, Seattle, WA
Collection: Artist

7 Sung Ho Choi
Photo of *American Pie,* 1996
Acrylic on panel, silk screen, plywood, 22 feet (diameter)
First Floor Ceiling of Public School I.S. 5 (Walter Crowley School) at 50-40 Jacobus Street, Queens, NY
Collection: Artist

8 Sook Jin Jo
News article of Installation *Color of Life* at the Socrates Sculptural Park, 2000 in *KoreAm Magazine,* 2003
Courtesy of the Artist

9 Sook Jin Jo
News article of a public art project during her Sacatar Foundation residency fellowship in Brazil in *Illinois Alumni,* 2002
Courtesy of the Artist

10 Jung Hyang Kim's Public Art Project for the MTA Station, Crescent Street (Jamaica Line), 2006
MTA Arts for Transit
Photography of Ken Shung
Courtesy of the Artist

**Plate G-3** Diagram of Art Works with Captions of "Theme 5: Looking Ahead for the Next Century 1990s" of *Coloring Time*

# Looking Ahead for the Next Century 1990s

A major trend in the 1990s was interest in public art or audience - engaged art. With more exhibition venues for minority artists, Korean - American artists became quite visible at public art institutions as well - for example, Whitney Museum of American Art showed works of Ik - joong Kang, Byron Kim, Y.David Chung as well as Nam June Paik. Theresa Hak Kyung Cha (1951 - 1982) continuously received —Ik-joong Kang, Soo-cheon Jheon, Inkie Whang, and Mo Bahc (Yiso Bahc) –ware selected to represent Korea at the Venice Biennale since 1995.

Sung Ho Choi, Sook Jin Jo, Mikyung Kim, Daru-Jung Hyang Kim, and Ik-Joong Kang continue to show large - scale works in public space or galleries. In the late 1990s and the 2000s, the generation born in the 1970s would join them and introduce a wide range of styles such as video art, photography, mixed media, performance, documentary films and other new forms-looking aheas for the 21st century.

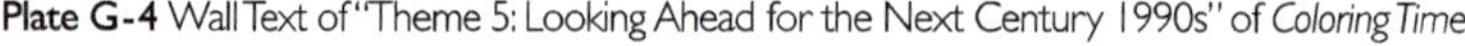

**Plate G-4** Wall Text of "Theme 5: Looking Ahead for the Next Century 1990s" of *Coloring Time*

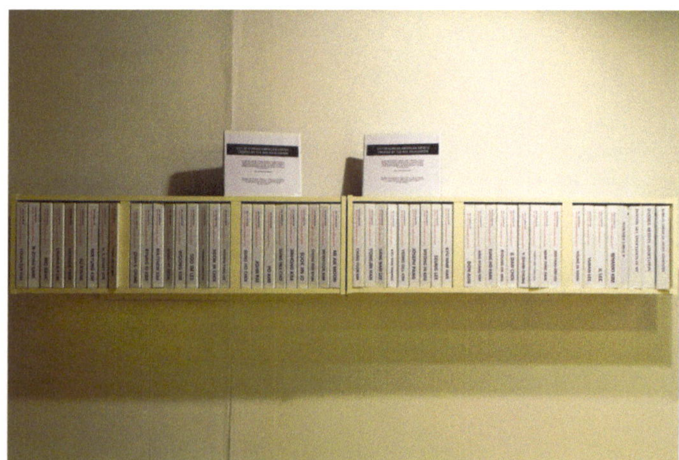

**Plate H** Photograph of Folders of the Archive of Korean-American Artists (AKAA)

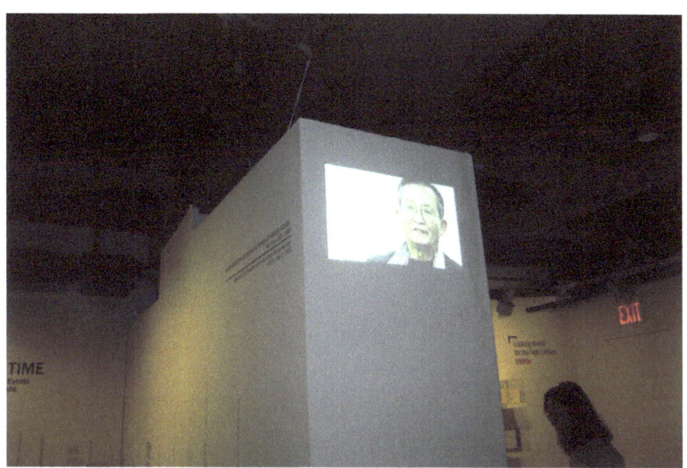


**Plate 1-1**
Photograph of Documentary Films on Korean-American Artists (Small Screen): Choong Sup Lim and Chong Gon Byun

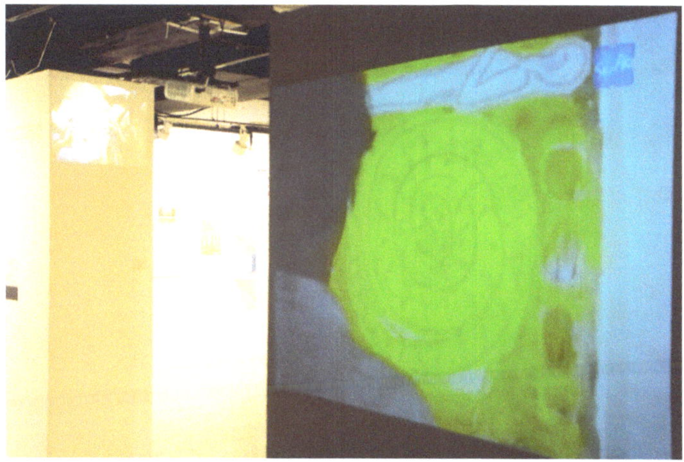

**Plate 1-2**
Photograph of Documentary Films on Korean-American Artists (Large Screen): Po Kim and Sook Jin Jo

**Chung Sup Lim**
Choong Sup Lim, *Luna and her Thousand Reflections,* 2012. 2 min 55 sec
Courtesy of National Museum of Contemporary Art, Korea
Choong Sup Lim, *Wol-In-Cheon-Ji,* 2012. 1 min 58
Courtesy of National Museum of Contemporary Art, Korea

**Chong Gon Byun**
Documentary of *BYUN,* part of a series *This Must Be the Place,* 2011. 4 min 21 sec
Produced and directed by Ben Wu and David Usui of Lost & Found Films
Courtesy of the Artist

Documentary of *BYUN, Object Trouvé,* 2012. 7 min
Produced and directed by Marie Losier
Courtesy of Marie Losier and the Artist

**Chang Seung Jung**
Recording of an exhibition at Minor Injury, 1991. 17 min 34 sec
Chan Seung Jun appears with his friends during an open studio for *Dialogue of Friendship* curated by Soo Kim in July 1991.
Courtesy of Julie Kim and Jae Wee

**Sook Jin Jo**
Recording of Installation for *Crossroads,* 2008. 4 min 36 sec
Courtesy of the artist
Recording of Installation for *Fantasy in D minor: Space Between II,* 2011. 6 min 16 sec
Courtesy of the artist

**Po Kim**
Documentary Film on Po Kim, 2010. 28 min 12 sec
Courtesy of the Sylvia Wald and Po Kim Art Gallery

**Plate I-3** Captions of Documentary Films on Korean-American Artists

# SELECTED BIBLIOGRAPHY


Archer, Michael. *Art Since 1960*. New York: Thames and Hudson, 2002

Ashton, Dore. *The New York School*. Berkeley: University of California Press, 1992.

Calo, Mary Ann, ed. *Critical Issues in American Art: A Book of Readings*. Boulder, CO: Westview Press, 1998.

Chae, Youngsuk. *Politicizing Asian American Literature: Towards a Critical Multiculturalism*. New York: Routledge, 2008.

Chang, Alexandra. *Envisioning Diaspora: Asian American Visual Arts Collectives from Godzilla, Godzookie to the Barnstormers*. Beijing: Timezone 8 Editions, 2009.

Chang, Gordon H., et al. *Asian American Art: A history 1850–1970*. Stanford: Stanford University Press, 2008.

Chiu, Melissa, and Benjamin Genocchio. *Contemporary Art in Asia: A Critical Reader*. Cambridge, MA and London: The MIT Press, 2011.

____________. *One Way or Another: Asian American Art Now*. New Haven and London: Asia Society with Yale University Press, 2006.

Chung Hyung-min. *Modern Korean Ink Painting*. Elizabeth, NJ and Seoul: Hollym, 2006.

Ciclitira, Serenella, ed. *Korean Eye: Contemporary Korean Art*. Milan: Skira; New York: Rizzoli International, 2010.

Cohen-Solal, Annie. *Leo and His Circle: The Life of Leo Castelli* New York: Alfred A. Knopf, 2010.

Cornell, Daniell, et al. *Asian American Modern Art: Shifting Currents, 1900–1970*. San Francisco, Fine Arts Museums of San Francisco; Berkeley, University of California Press, 2008.

Dodds, Jane, and Cathleen Crabb. *Project DMZ*. New York: Storefront for Art and Architecture (97 Kenmare St., New York 10012), 1988.

Dompierre, Louise, et al. *Fast Forward: The Vibrant Art Scene of the Republic of Korea*. Toronto: Power Plant, 1997.

Enwezor, Okwui. *Archive Fever: Uses of the Document in Contemporary Art*. New York: International Center of Photography; Gottingen: Steidl, 2008.

*Faces & Facts: Contemporary Korean Art in New York—Celebrating the 30th Anniversary of the Korean Cultural Service New York*. New York: Korean Cultural Service, 2009.

Faver, Jane. *Across the Pacific: Contemporary Korean and Korean American Art*. New York: Queens Museum of Art in cooperation with SEORO Korean Cultural Network, 1993.

____________, *et al. Global Conceptualism: Points of Origin, 1950s–1980s*. New York: Queens Museum of Art, 1999.

Foster, Hal, et al. *Art Since 1990: 1945 to the Present*. Vol. 2. New York: Thames and Hudson, 2004.

Gallery Korea. *Green Light: Twenty Young Korean Artists in New York*. New York: Korean Cultural Service, 2004.

Gelburd, *Gail, et al. The Trans Parent Thread: Asian Philosophy in Recent American Art*. Hempstead, NY: Hofstra University and Bard College, 1990; distributed by University of Pennsylvania Press.

Greenberg, Clement, and John O'Brian. *Clement Greenberg: The Collected Essays and Criticism, Modernism with a Vengeance 1957–1969*. Chicago: University of Chicago Press, 1993.

Hanhardt, John G. *The Worlds of Nam June Paik*. New York: Guggenheim Museum, 2000.

Herskovic, Marika. *The New York School Abstract Expressionists: Artists Choice by Artists*. New York: New York School Press, 2000.

Hopkins, David. *After Modern Art 1945–2000*. Oxford: Oxford University Press, 2000.

Kaiser, Philipp, and Miwon Kwon. *Ends of the Earth: Land Art to 1974*. Munich and New York: Prestel, 2012.

Kee, Joan. "Points, Lines, Encounters, Worlds: Tansaekhwa and the Formation of Contemporary Korean Art." Ph.D. dissertation, New York University, 2008.

Kim, Elaine H. *Asian American Literature: An Introduction to the Writings and their Social Context*. Philadelphia: Temple University Press, 1982.

____________, and Chungmoo Choi. *Dangerous Women: Gender and Korean Nationalism*. New York: Routledge, 1998.

____________, Margo Machida, and Sharon Mizota. *Fresh Talk, Daring Gazes: Conversations on Asian American Art. Berkeley:* University of California Press, 2003.

__________, et al., eds. *Making More Waves: New Writing by Asian American Women.* Boston: Beacon Press, 1997.

__________, and Janice Otani. *With Silk Wings: Asian American Women at Work.* San Francisco: Asian Women United of California, 1983.

Kim, Miki Wick. *Korean Contemporary Art.* Munich: Prestel, 2012.

Kim, Youngna. *Modern and Contemporary Art in Korea: Tradition, Modernity, and Identity.* Elizabeth, NJ and Seoul: Hollym, 2005.

__________. *20th Century Korean Art.* London: King Laurence Publishing, 2006.

Kim, Yu Yeon. *Korea Transfer: 13 Contemporary Korean Artists in New York.* New York: Korean Cultural Service, 2006.

Kim, Laura, and Wei Ming Dariotis. *War baby/Love Child: Mixed Race Asian American Art.* Seattle: University of Washington Press, 2013.

Machida, Margo, Vishaka Desai, and John Tchen. *Asia/America: Identities in contemporary Asian American Art.* New York: Asia Society Galleries and New Press, 1994.

Machida, Margo. *Unsettled Visions: Contemporary Asian American Artists and the Social Imaginary.* Durham, NC: Duke University Press, 2008.

Marcoci, Roxana, Diana Murphy, and Eve Sinaiko, eds. *New Art.* New York: Abrams, 1997.

Min, Pyong Gap, ed. *Asian Americans: Contemporary Trends and Issues.* London: SAGE Publications, 2006.

Morgan, Robert C. *The End of the Art World.* New York: Allworth Press, 1998.

Munroe, Alexandra. *The Third Mind : American Artists Contemplate Asia*, 1860–1989. New York: Guggenheim Museum, 2009.

Pal, Pratapaditya. *American Collectors of Asian Art.* Bombay: Marg Publications, 1986.

Park, Edward J. W., and John S. W. Park. *Probationary Americans: Contemporary Immigration Policies and the Shaping of Asian American Communities.* New York: Routledge, 2005.

Park, J.P *Keeping It Real: Korean Artists in the Age of Multi-Media Representation.* Boulder, CO: University of Colorado Art Museum and Seoul: Workroom Press, 2012.

Park, John S. W. *Elusive Citizenship: Immigration, Asian Americans, and the Paradox of Civil Rights.* New York: New York University Press, 2004.

Perry, Gill, and Paul Wood. *Themes in Contemporary Art.* New Haven: Yale University Press, 2004.

Poon, Irene. *Leading the Way: Asian American Artists of the Older Generation.* Wenham, MA: Gordon College, 2001.

Roe, Jae-Ryung. "The Representation of National Identity in Korean Art Exhibitions, 1951–1994." Ph.D. dissertation, New York University, 1995.

Rosati, Lauren, and Anne Staniszewski. *Alternative Histories: New York Art Spaces, 1960 to 2010.* Cambridge, MA: MIT Press, 2013.

Schaffner, Ingrid. *Deep Storage: Collecting, Storing, and Archiving in Art.* Munich and New York: Prestel, 1998.

Schwarz, Arturo. *The Complete Works of Marcel Duchamp.* London: Thames and Hudson, 1969

Seitz, William C. *The Art of Assemblage*, exhibition catalog. New York: The Museum of Modern Art, 1961.

Sinsheimer, Karen, et al. *Chaotic Harmony: Contemporary Korean Photography.* Houston: Museum of Fine Arts and Santa Barbara: Santa Barbara Museum of Art, 2009; distributed by Yale University Press.

Starkman, Christine, ed. *Your Bright Future: 12 Contemporary Artists from Korea.* Houston, Museum of Fine Arts; Los Angeles: Los Angeles County Museum of Art, 2009; distributed by Yale University Press.

Stiles, Kristen, and Peter Selz, eds. *Theories and Documents of Contemporary Art: A Sourcebook of Artists'* Writings. Berkeley: University of California Press, 1996.

Taylor, Brandon. *Contemporary Art Since 1970.* London: Laurence King Publishing, 2004.

Taylor, Marvin J. *The Downtown Book: The New York Art Scene, 1974–1984.* Princeton: Princeton University Press, 2006.

Thompson, Don. *The $12 Million Stuffed Shark: The Curious Economics of Contemporary Art.* New York: Palgrave Macmillan, 2008.

Tiampo, Ming, and Alexandra Munroe. *Gutai: Splendid Playground.* New York: Guggenheim Museum, 2013.

Tsutakawa, Mayumi et al. *They Painted from their Hearts: Pioneer Asian American Artists*. Seattle : Wing Luke Asian Museum, 1994.

Turner, Fred. "The Family of Man and the Politics of Attention in Cold War America." *Public Culture* 24: 1 (2012): 55-84.

Wechsler, Michael, ed. *Asian Traditions/Modern Expressions: Asian American Artists and Abstraction, 1945–1970.* East Brunswick, NJ: Jane Voorhees Zimmerli Art Museum at the State University of New Jersey, Rutgers, 1997.

Yang, Alice. Why Asia?: *Contemporary Asian and Asian American Art.* New York: New York University Press, 1998.

# NOTES ON CONTRIBUTORS

**Hee Sung Cho**
She is a curator of Gallery Korea at the Korean Cultural Service New York.

**Soojung Hyun**
She is an independent curator and chief researcher for the Archive of Korean-American Artists at the AHL Foundation. Dr. Hyun has lived in New York since 2007 and organized several shows as a curator. She was invited as a juror for the Tehran Contemporary Sculpture Biennale (2007). She worked as a curator for an exhibition, "Breathing" (2011) and was an organizer for the "East Village Forum" (2010 and 2011), both for the Sylvia Wald & Po Kim Art Gallery in New York. She is currently a member of the gallery's advisory board. She graduated from Chonnam National University and then received a Ph.D. at Chosun University in Gwang-ju, Korea. She also studied at the Art Students League in New York.

**Sook Nyu Lee Kim**
She is the president of AHL Foundation.

**Woo Sung Lee**
He is the director of Korean Cultural Service New York.

**Kyunghee Pyun**
She is an assistant professor at State University of New York, Fashion Institute ofTechnology. She has also worked as a visiting assistant professor in the department of history of art and design at Pratt Institute, Brooklyn, NY. She has been publishing on topics related to Asian-American visual culture and reception of Asian art in Europe and North America. She has written "Asian Art in the Eyes of American Collectors, 1880–1920: Antimodernism and Exotic Desire" was written for *Journal of Contemporary Art Studies* 15 no. 2 (2011): 245–278 and a book review of *Contemporary Art in Asia: A Critical Reader* edited by Melissa Chiu and Benjamin Genocchio (Cambridge MA and London: The MIT Press, 2011) for a forthcoming issue ofTiger's Eye: Bilingual Journal on Contemporary Art and Theory. She has organized a session entitled Rethinking "Influences" of Modern Art in Korea: Beyond Colonial Discourses at the Association for Asian Studies Annul Conference in 2009, which became part of her new book, Modern Art on the Asian Soil: Practicing Western Art 1880–2000. She graduated from Seoul National University and received an M.A. and Ph.D. at the Institute of Fine Arts, New York University.

**Deborah Saleeby-Mulligan**
She has been a visiting and adjunct professor in the department of art history at Manhattanville College, Purchase, NY. Her book *Painting the Irish Conflict: The Belfast Murals of Gerard Mo chara Kelly* was published in 2009. Her article, "Painting the Irish Conflict: The Street Murals of Belfast and Derry as Expressions of a Warn-Torn Community" was written for *Chicago Art Review* in 2005. As specialist of African and Irish contemporary art, she used to work as archivist in the department of the Arts of Africa, Oceania, and the Americas at the Metropolitan Museum of Art. She graduated from Long Island University, received an M.A. from Hunter College and a Ph.D. from the Graduate School and University Center, City University of New York.

# ACKNOWLEDGMENTS

Many people have been involved in the Archive of Korean-American Artists project. About forty or so artists contributed their personal documents, materials, drawings, photographs, and works of art to this exhibition. When asked to submit early works made shortly after their arrival in the 1960s or 1970s, some artists regretted that their works from those valuable years did not survive well; lack of space or technical expertise for preserving these works were often the reasons. This project has raised the awareness of these artists that their working processes in fact provide a valuable addition to art history.

Ms. Sook Nyu Lee Kim, president of the AHL Foundation secured funding and overwhelming support among board members. She also lent several art works from her private collection, and donated her business records as the owner of the Hankook Gallery in the 1970s and 1980s. Although she is neither an art critic nor a scholar, she has been a precious repository of numerous anecdotes and details about Korean and Korean-American artists in the United States. She had met many artists when she ran Hankook Gallery and started the AHL Foundation.

Ms. Eunyoung Kang, the chair of the AHL Foundation's board also lent works from her own collection, and encouraged other collectors to contribute to our exhibition. She sometimes had to lead us in midst of chaos, but thanks to her, we have been able to streamline our exhibition and stay focused. Ms. Kang and other board members have shown unfailing support of this project. I thank them very much.

Mr. Woo Sung Lee, director of the Korean Cultural Service New York, has been generous in making this exhibition a success. Ms. Hee Sung Cho and her staff worked tirelessly to keep me informed and provide old records of exhibitions held at the Korean Cultural Service and Gallery Korea. Ms. Eunyoung Kang designed wall texts and labels for the exhibition while Ms. Juhea Kim added her effort to complicated installation of art works and archive materials. Mr. Kevin Park, art director at the Metropolitan Museum of Art, also deserves my sincerest thanks for sharing his professional wisdom with us. Thanks to his keen advice, Curator Hee Sung Cho and I were able to focus limited resources on the most vital elements of the exhibition.

Dr. Soojung Hyun, chief researcher of the Archive of Korean-American Artists at the AHL Foundation, added her enthusiasm and special charm to the project. Her advocacy on promoting public art within the history of Korean contemporary art gained a place for public art projects by Korean-American artists at the end of this exhibition.

Our interns, Mr. Wonseok Choi and Ms. Jongsook Ko, put in endless hours, sometimes as curatorial assistant and sometimes as photographers, documenting and updating records for the archive and the exhibition. The list of Korean-American artists in progress is a product of Ms. Goh's hard work. Many photographs in the catalogue and in the exhibition are works produced by Mr. Choi. We thank them for their hard work and devotion.

Graphic designer of the AHL Foundation, Ms. Jieun Yim, who has created this handsome catalogue for this exhibition, was incredibly resourceful to be able to present several proposals within a tight schedule. We are all tremendously grateful for her dedication to the project.

Among the many artists who took time to answer our questions, sort out their old records, tour their studios, and provide art works or drawings for our project, Mr. Sung-ho Choi deserves special thanks. A fastidious organizer of all kinds of records, he not only had two or three copies of the same document or record of himself, but also kept records for his friends. Most of our materials on the 1980s and 1990s are drawn from Mr. Choi's personal archive. Indeed, he needs to plan an exhibition or publish a catalogue on his immense compendium of letters, photographs, catalogues, posters, and meeting minutiae. I am touched by his generosity in sharing his materials with us and making them accessible to public.

Dr. Matthew Kim, a renowned collector of Whanki Kim and other Korean artists, gave us a precious interview. It is fortunate that he published his memoir before the exhibition was open. Mr. Sung Ho Choi was one of the most pivotal figures in creating the Archive of Korean-American Artists and realizing this exhibition. Most archival records for the 1980s and 1990s came from his personal collection. He not only organized documents and records for himself, but also generously accumulated reviews and catalogues for his friends. Mr. Yong-jin Han gave us a rare glimpse of his and his wife's studios during a short visit to the United States from his current home on Je-ju Island, Korea. Mr. Po Kim took the time to tell us of his experiences as a disoriented youth on foreign soil. Ms. Youn-hee Paik organized a splendid gathering of old friends to meet young researchers like us. The following artists all welcomed us to their studios and provided crucial information: Sook Jin Jo, Chong Gon Byun, Yeong Gill Kim, Tchah-sup Kim, Chong Yun Kim, Byung-ok Min, Soo Im Lee, Choong Sup Lim, Il Dan Choi, Mikyung Kim, Woong Kim, Ik-joong Kang, and Myong Hi Kim. Some artists who had passed away had dear family members who helped us discover more materials and records. It is unfortunate that we did not have time to include more artists beyond our reach. The Archive of Korean-American Artists will continue to work with them.

I also thank the staff at Asia Art Archive, the National Museum of Contemporary Art in Korea, the Museum of Modern Art, the Whitney Museum of American Art, the Guggenheim Museum, the Queens Museum of Art, and the Brooklyn Museum.

Ms. Barbara Magalnick edited this catalogue with enormous passion. Dr. Deborah Saleeby-Mulligan, who had a very tight schedule, nonetheless wrote a beautiful essay. I am very pleased that she was able to contribute to this catalogue. Finally I would like to thank my supportive family for understanding my absentmindedness during this period.

# COLORING TIME

An Exhibition from the Archive of Korean - American Artists

Part One

(1955 - 1989)

Kyunghee Pyun, Editor

AHL FOUNDATION, INC.

www.ingramcontent.com/pod-product-compliance
Lightning Source LLC
LaVergne TN
LVHW070131110826
845147LV00002B/231

* 9 7 8 0 9 8 9 0 3 7 8 0 8 *